Digging The Wells of Revival

Reclaiming Your Historic Inheritance
Through Prophetic Intercession

Lou Engle

with Catherine Paine

Endorsements

"Lou Engle is the most fervent prayer warrior I have ever met in my life. He has faithfully prayed over many years to see what we now see in the moving of God's Spirit today. This book will challenge you to lay hold of God at a whole new level."

John Arnott, Senior Pastor
Toronto Airport Christian Fellowship

"Lou Engle's passion, displayed in *Digging the Wells of Revival*, will motivate you to seek God in reclaiming the spiritual heritage that will bring revival in your heart."

Ted Haggard, Senior Pastor
New Life Church

"There are few prophetic men of prayer I know like Lou Engle. For more than 15 years, we have walked together as friends seeking the presence of the Lord and revival for our city. I believe that he has heard the voice of God in writing this book—and that it is an urgent sound that Los Angeles and the nation need to hear right now to further release the waters of revival."

Dr. Ché Ahn, Senior Pastor
Harvest Rock Church
President of Harvest International Ministries

"Lou Engle is one of the true flame throwers of intercession in the Body of Christ today! The inspiration of his life and the teaching of this book will instill in you a love for Church history and challenge you to be a consuming fire called the 'house of prayer for all nations.' "

Jim W. Goll, Founder
Ministry to the Nations
Author of *The Lost Art of Intercession*

"This is a crucial book for this critical hour. Like a prophet of old, my good friend, Lou Engle, boldly encourages us to lay hold of the inheritance we have in our forefathers who ushered in the great revivals of the past. It happened then and it can happen now! The anointing of the past has always been our destiny for today. *Digging the Wells of Revival* is a must-read book for intercessors and for all of us who are desperate to see revival come."

Wesley Campbell, Pastor
New Life Vineyard Fellowship
Director of Revival Now! Ministries

"*Digging the Wells of Revival* is a historic book. The message is revelatory and much needed for the whole prayer movement. Lou Engle has tapped into the new move of God."

Cindy Jacobs, Co-Founder
Generals of Intercession

"If people will read and act on the mandate in this book, the Church and the world will change."

Kathy Miller, Writer
Destiny Image Publishers

Dedication

This book is first dedicated to the memory of those pioneers of the faith in Los Angeles who, through sacrificial prayer and obedience, opened up rivers of the Holy Spirit for thousands to drink from—fathers and mothers like Frank Bartleman, Aimee Semple McPherson, and John Wimber, upon whose shoulders a new generation in Los Angeles now stands.

Secondly, I owe such a debt to my own father and mother, Gordon and Eunice Engle, who released such a godly inheritance upon me. Your prayers and altars took hold of my life at an early age. May I be graced to raise up such a godly seed as you have done.

Ché, what a friend and comrade. Your faith in me and your encouragement have carried me forward. I wouldn't have made it under any other pastor. Revival in Los Angeles!

Most of all, I give thanks to my wife, Therese, my "Hallelujah lassie," who has believed in me, prayed for me, and put up with my fasting and the quirks of an intercessor. You have given me a foundation from which to write this book by pouring yourself selflessly into our children, Christy Joy, Jesse, Josiah, Jonathan, Gloria, and Jacob. Children, may you rise up and dig the well of your father and mother.

Finally, I dedicate this book to the original and ultimate Father, my heavenly Father. Thank You for Your covenants of love released to my fathers and for calling me to sonship. I cry, "Abba, Father."

Acknowledgments

I would like to wholeheartedly thank Catherine Paine and Bessie Watson for praying this book into being, provoking me to express in writing all that the Lord has given me, and helping me write and edit this manuscript. Thanks to Ken and Val Storey, my fellow well diggers; Ray and Melinda Clarke, my radical friends; Ferne Heyerdahl, a great secretary; and Chris Berglund, my man of the open Heaven.

To the Rock of Roseville Church—Your generosity helped pave the way to finance writing this message. Thanks! Thank you to all the pastors of Harvest Rock Church. How God has knit us together is a marvelous wonder. Thank you to all the faithful intercessors of Harvest Rock Church for your tireless prayer—you are greatly esteemed in Heaven!

Foreword

Within our history lies our hope. *Digging the Wells of Revival* draws our attention to the spiritual inheritance of our country. From Azusa Street in Los Angeles at the turn of this century, to Toronto, Baltimore, and Brownsville as we face the next century, Lou Engle reminds us that what was, can be what is—where waters once flowed freely, they can again spring forth in this generation.

In this book, Lou Engle challenges us to revisit the landmarks, renew the commitments, redig the wells, and let revival and anointing break forth as never before. Is it happening? I think I see a trickle!

I have lived and worked among praying people all my life. I am a man of prayer myself. Lou Engle, however, is without a doubt the praying-est man I've ever known! Hand me a shovel, Lou—I'm ready to dig!

Tommy Tenney
Revival Evangelist

Contents

Introduction

I do not consider myself an author. But like many other things God does, He does not choose the most qualified. God gave me a message and a mandate that so burns within me that I had no other choice but to write it. I have an overpowering sense of the urgency of the hour we live in. Like King Josiah, we are living on borrowed time, when judgment is withheld only if the covenant is renewed.

My hope is that this book will call the Church to return to the spiritual heritage and prayer pursuits of their forefathers and mothers and to redig the wells of revival, rather than reap the destruction of judgment.

God wants to awaken every one of His sons and daughters to their spiritual inheritance. He stands ready to release to us the anointing, glory, and power from days gone by...and more. He waits to visit us again as He has in revivals past, sweeping multitudes into His arms and filling our streets and homes with His presence.

He stands ready to honor His covenants afresh with the fathers and mothers of the faith who have gone before us, and to pass on to us the riches of our spiritual heritage if we but ask and seek for it.

What I have written has been birthed by my own "well digging" experiences. As you read, may a great expectation arise in your heart to see the revival well that bubbles beneath your feet gush forth.

Perhaps you are a teacher in the Body of Christ in whom this book will awaken a passion and a commission to teach the

Church how to renew covenant with our God. May you grab the baton and take us all to the next level!

Maybe you know that you have a great destiny—yet you continually struggle to find your spiritual identity. May this book point you toward the answers you seek, and may it compel you to search out the riches of the spiritual inheritance God has for you *right now* and to walk in the promises for which He gave His life *for you*.

Whoever you are in the family of God, may this book take you higher, wider, and deeper into the knowledge of the Father's purpose for you, and into His plans to fill the whole earth with His glory. May you irrevocably become a catalyst for revival!

God asked me to sound the trumpet and pass out the shovels. I hope I have done that. The rest is up to you! Let's dig the wells!

Chapter 1

Jubilee or Judgment?

Tornadoes of Judgment

We were walking outside when torrential rain started to pour down. Huge drops of rain the size of golf balls fell all around us, yet we were not getting wet. Suddenly, we began to run. Ray shouted to me, "Look!" In the distance, not too far away, two tornadoes were coming toward us. To our left was a grand old mansion; our families were inside. We began to pray for the mansion and our families to be protected in Jesus' name.

Suddenly, we noticed that twisters were forming right above our heads. As we prayed, we were compelled to reach out and touch the twisters. The instant we made contact with them, the tornadoes dissipated and went back into the clouds. As more and more twisters came, we began to do full extension dives to intercept them before they touched the ground.

Timing was critical. At times, we dove and made the contact when only a space as wide as a man's hand stood between the twister and the ground. Again and again we dove, intercepting one tornado after another. Soon we noticed that our hands were burning from touching the tornadoes. Blisters began to form on our skin.

Overhead, dozens more tornadoes began to form. The sky was filled, and the twisters became too numerous to count. We exclaimed to each other at the top of our lungs, "Never before has this happened in history!" Oddly enough, we felt no fear...but stood in awe of the spectacle.

Right in the middle of this scene, we noticed a small child standing on the porch of the old mansion, weeping. No one came to console him as one normally would do for a child. We could not leave our assignment to go to him, either.

Then we began to notice an astounding phenomenon. Whenever we touched the earth or water as we were diving to stop the tornadoes, more twisters began to form—this time, from the ground up! Overcome with amazement and the fear of the Lord, we knew this was from God.

Somehow, God was allowing us to intervene. As we were diverting the tornadoes plummeting toward the earth, God was releasing twisters of water through us that arose from the ground. Only as we dove to stop the descending torrents could we initiate an ascending waterspout.

As my friend Ray told me his dream, my heart began to beat forcefully within me. Before he began to explain to me what he felt it meant, I already knew! The tornadoes represented the judgments that are soon to be released against Hollywood and my city of Los Angeles, while the tornadoes that formed from the ground up were the blessings of God through revival. The grand old mansion in the dream was the Church, a place of safety in the midst of calamity. Ray recognized the child praying on the porch as the son of a pastor friend. He was weeping "between the temple porch and the altar" (Joel 2:17) in intercession, not fear.

Only the day before, I had been crying out to the Lord in prayer to stay His hand of judgment on Los Angeles. As I returned from my early morning prayer time, my 11-year-old son, Jesse, met me with great soberness. "Dad," Jesse said, "I just woke up from a dream in which three tornadoes were coming toward Los Angeles. I knew they were the judgments of God. You and I ran for the prayer room at church, where I began to weep and cry out to the Lord, 'God, spare L.A. You've got to renew the covenants.' " I was stunned by Jesse's words. In his dream he had prayed the exact thing I had been praying that very morning in the prayer room as I had cried out, "God, spare L.A. You've got to renew the covenants."

Now here was Ray telling me virtually the same dream a day later. His dream had been so vivid and urgent that it had shaken him deeply. After much prayer and confirmation, he took a 40-day leave of absence from his job as a television editor in Hollywood, to join me to fast and pray for Los Angeles. When he told his sister, a non-Christian who also works in Hollywood, about his plans, she shared with him a terrifying dream she had just had where two tornadoes destroyed Hollywood! She tried to run for the mountains to escape, but could not. She said she had watched helplessly as the city burned.

God had my attention! He had been speaking to me about traveling and preaching less and giving myself to intercession for the city. These unusual events were all part of a convergence of prophetic words that the Lord has spoken over my life and in many ways are the reason for writing this book at this hour.

Your Place in the Vision

This is more than just a personal revelation, but a statement, a sign of the times, and an urgent prophetic mandate for the Church. This task is not for me alone, but for the many godly intercessors and leaders that God is raising up to meet the challenge of this critical hour. We are in a season unlike any other in the history of America. God is calling His intercessors to fast and pray like never before. There is an urgency about this commission to fall on our faces before the Lord. As Derek Prince writes, "In God's dealings with nations, His promises of blessing and His warnings of judgment are both alike: they are conditional. Judgment may be averted—even at the eleventh hour—by repentance. Conversely, blessing may be forfeited by disobedience."[1]

I believe we have entered a window of time in which our destiny is being decided. The court of Heaven is weighing the American Church in the balance. My own city, Los Angeles, has certainly seen its share of judgments from God in the past decade, including massive earthquakes, mudslides, firestorms that have raged uncontrollably on our hillsides, and riots in which people died and entire city blocks burned to the ground.

At the moment, there seems to be a lull before the storm. You may even feel it in your own life, city, or ministry. More accurately, I believe it is a window of opportunity…a window that won't last forever. What we do now is critical to determining the outcome of history for the nation and the Church.

Assessing the Hour

Cities and nations seem to reach a critical point after which revival and judgment follow closely—often hand in hand. To those who witnessed the terrible San Francisco earthquake of 1906, in which more than ten thousand people were killed, it was no coincidence that the physical earthquake came within days of the spiritual revival that broke out on Azusa Street in Los Angeles and rocked the nations. From it were birthed the Pentecostal and later the Charismatic movements that changed the face of Christianity and the world.

Frank Bartleman, a principal leader in the Azusa Street Revival, recorded his thoughts as it happened:

"I felt a deep conviction that the Lord was answering our prayers for a revival in His own way. 'When Thy judgments are in the earth, the inhabitants of the world learn righteousness.'—Isa. 26:9. A tremendous burden of prayer came upon me that the people might not be indifferent to His voice….

"The San Francisco earthquake was surely the voice of God to the people on the Pacific Coast. ... In the early 'Azusa' days both Heaven and hell seemed to have come to town. Men were at the breaking point. ... When men came within two or three blocks of the place [Azusa Street] they were seized with conviction."[2]

America appears to be entering such a season again. The alarm clocks of history are sounding and sirens are blaring if we have ears to hear. Will it be Jubilee, or will it be judgment? Just consider:

- This year, 1998, marks the 50th anniversary of the birth of the nation of Israel and the literal Jewish year of Jubilee.

- A massive reawakening of prayer and fasting is taking place—much like the great movement begun more than 50 years ago when Franklin Hall wrote *Atomic Power With God Through Prayer and Fasting* in 1946.

- We are right in the middle of the "Jubilee year" commemorating the 1947–1949 worldwide outpouring of the Holy Spirit that gave rise to the healing revivals of the Latter Day Rain, the campus revivals spearheaded by Bill Bright, and the release of great evangelists like Billy Graham.

The reestablishment of the nation of Israel in particular released spiritual shock waves into the heavenlies 50 years ago that are still reverberating throughout the earth. The spiritual and natural ramifications of this Jubilee year cannot be underestimated.

Likewise, it is no coincidence that Bill Bright, founder of Campus Crusade in the late 1940's, came under a tremendous burden in 1995 and 1996—50 years later—that the future of America was hanging in the balance. In the midst of a 40-day fast, God spoke to him and said that the greatest harvest in the history of America would be brought in before the year 2001 if God's people would humble themselves in prayer and fasting.

Compelled by this prophetic insight, Bright wrote the book, *The Coming Revival: America's Call to Fast, Pray, and "Seek God's Face,"* which has released an unprecedented, cross-denominational wave of fasting in America. The book comes 50 years after Franklin Hall's book shared a similar call.

Is this coincidence or the schematic hand of a faithful and purposeful Creator? Likewise, how do we assess that 50 years after the outpourings of the Holy Spirit in 1948, reports again flood in describing healing revivals all over the world?

God has indeed released His covenant promise of Jubilee, or unprecedented blessing, in this season. Will it remain in blessing...or end in judgment?

The Purpose of Jubilee

Every fiftieth year, God commands a Jubilee: "Consecrate the fiftieth year and proclaim liberty throughout the land to all its inhabitants. It shall be a jubilee for you..." (Lev. 25:10). In the Jubilee year, the land was to be given complete rest—no sowing, reaping, or harvesting was permitted, although the people could gather what grew up naturally. Jewish slaves and their families were to be set free. Family inheritances of land that had been lost through poverty, or had not been redeemed, were to revert to the original owners or rightful heirs, and all debts were cancelled. It was a year that culminated seven Sabbath seasons—that is, the years of rest that came at the end of every seven-year period.

America has the opportunity to move into the fullness of such a period of grace and restoration. It is now an hour when we can move with God to restore what has been lost in our society. Where we have forfeited our rightful inheritance, in this day of favor, we can reclaim it. We can once again possess the blessings that are rightfully ours. We must move with God in the favorable day, as He instructs us in Isaiah 49:8: "This is what the Lord says: 'In the time of My favor I will answer you, and in the day of salvation I will help you; I will keep you and will make you to be a covenant for the people, to restore the land and to reassign its desolate inheritances.'"

Yet even in a time of blessing can come calamity. Isaiah 61:1-2 declares,

> *The Spirit of the Sovereign Lord is on me, because the Lord has anointed me to preach good news to the poor. He has sent me to bind up the brokenhearted, to proclaim freedom for the captives and release from darkness for the prisoners, to proclaim the year of the Lord's favor and the day of vengeance of our God....*

I am struck by the latter part of verse 2: "and the day of *vengeance* of our God...." I cannot help but consider how this warning fits into the crux of timing for our nation, particularly in light of an article I read in *Intercessors for America*. This article grabbed my attention because it warned of an impending mile marker for our nation. America was founded on covenant, with a federal (from the Latin for "covenant") constitution. The writer states that the Bible used covenants "as a means of showing mercy and giving protection to someone who did not deserve it. A nation's covenant, its highest law, provides a means of mercy and protection to the people of the land if it is based on godly principles. But when a nation breaks the covenant, it is no longer protected. It falls under God's judgement and wrath."[3]

Scripture shows that God deals with Gentile nations in 70-year cycles.[4] As the writer notes, America's first cycle began when Virginia ratified the Bill of Rights, thereby completing our constitutional covenant. At the end of this cycle came the seeds of civil war. But Lincoln and others upheld the covenant, and our nation was restored. The next cycle ended in 1929 when the stock market crashed. But people were humbled and God had mercy on our nation. Yet the author concludes, "This nation's third generation will end in December, 1998. If America is called to account for this generation's sins, will God be able to show us covenant mercy even in the midst of judgement?"[5]

I was shaken as I read these words. It is far more than chance that the year of Jubilee and the day of reckoning for America's third generation coincide. Could it be that both the year of the favor of the Lord and the day of vengeance of our God are upon us? Might it be that our prayers and obedience can yet determine the outcome?

One City in the Balance

The options for one city—my city—seem quite clear. The prophetic words for Los Angeles from major leaders across the Body of Christ are consistent and foreboding. There is a storm approaching. America is going to be called to account for the filth she has embraced and the covenant with God she has rejected. And it may begin with destruction in Los Angeles. Rick Joyner, Bob Jones, and other well-known prophets have all spoken of a massive earthquake that is coming to Los Angeles.

> "There are many cities and regions that are about to experience God's judgments. However, I do not believe that the judgment coming to the Los Angeles area has as much to do with the degree of evil as it does the ability to project evil and send it around the world. No other city in our time has caused more people to stumble than Los Angeles, mostly for what has come out of Hollywood. This will not continue much longer, either because of repentance or because of destruction."[6]

Los Angeles stands in a true gate of hell—there is a flood of filth coming out of this city. I wish I could say this wasn't true. But all evidence points to the contrary—especially an article in the *Los Angeles Daily News*, entitled "Porn Pays." It states that sales and rentals of adult videos have doubled in five years, up from $2.1 billion annually to $4.2 billion. In just 1997 alone, 700 million adult tapes were rented. By contrast, only 410 million were rented in 1991. A chief economist for the Economic Development Corporation of Los Angeles County acknowledged in the same article that the San Fernando Valley is the porn capitol of the world.[7]

The tragic fact is that many in the Church are themselves in some addiction to pornography. With what authority can we call a city to repent if we as Christians are feeding on the same sin? Rick Joyner continues,

> "Judgment is about to come to southern California because the spiritual pollution coming from there is poisoning the whole earth. It is very close to reaching the limit of what can be tolerated. If a profound repentance does not come, much of the Los Angeles basin will be destroyed to the point where the ocean will lap at the base of the mountains in Pasadena. The buildings in downtown Los Angeles will sink into the earth like stones in a jar of sand when it is shaken.[8]
>
> "Again, God does not want this to happen. He always prefers mercy over judgment, but there is a point when His judgment will be mercy. … We do not know at what point the Lord will relent and spare Los Angeles, but there is a delusion in much of the church that is presuming on God's grace. Some have been spiritualizing the prophecies, saying that the shaking that is coming is spiritual, and that the water [that] will cover Los Angeles speaks of coming revival. What I was shown was not a spiritual earthquake, and the waters were the Pacific Ocean. However, if such a spiritual shaking did take place, and such a revival did come to Los Angeles, the literal earthquake will still come, but its damage could be greatly reduced. I intended to pray for mercy until the actual judgment comes.
>
> "Pride comes before the fall, and there is an arrogance toward the Lord that has even permeated much of the church in southern California. One way that this is manifested is the disregard for His warnings (which He sent in the previous quake [the 1996 Northridge earthquake]), and the tendency to believe that they can be handled. No one will think this after the one that is coming, even if its destructive power is reduced. At its lowest level, the fear of the Lord will pass across the earth just as the tidal

waves that will go out from it. Repentance and intercession can remove a lot of the death and destruction, but this earthquake is going to be a big one.

"...He [God] also showed me that it can be delayed if we will honor the fathers and mothers of the faith from that region who have so powerfully blessed our nation. The commandment to honor our fathers and mothers has the promise that if we do, our days will be long upon the earth. If we will '[dig] again the wells' (Genesis 26:18) of our spiritual fathers and mothers and continue to drink from them, it will honor them and the Lord will give us more time.

"However, the Lord has often given us more time to get ready, but we have rarely used time well. ..."9

I was spiritually pierced through by these words. *Something in my heart leaped to hear the call to redig the wells of revival dug by our spiritual forefathers and to drink from the cup of covenant and blessing that they had enjoyed before God.*

I have been standing in the gap for Los Angeles for 14 years, seeking to do this very thing! God is now calling for intercessors everywhere to redig the ancient wells and stand in the gap for our cities. He is putting forth a plea—*and a commission*—for the sake of our children, our nation, and the future.

The alternative that God spoke in Ezekiel 22 must not be:

I looked for a man among them who would build up the wall and stand before Me in the gap on behalf of the land so I would not have to destroy it, but I found none. So I will pour out My wrath on them and consume them with My fiery anger, bringing down on their own heads all they have done, declares the Sovereign Lord (Ezekiel 22:30-31).

Our presence or absence in this gap is the deciding factor for our cities. We must pick up the mantle and obey. God is raising up intercessors who will run into the gap, postpone the judgment, and renew the covenant. We must not let our cities become like Sodom and Gomorrah![10]

The destruction that befell these cities ultimately came not because of the great wickedness of the people, but because they lacked even ten righteous men! *They lacked a revival core—an intercessory band of holy men and women who relentlessly petition the throne of God on behalf of their city, and whose very lives have a purifying and preserving quality*, like the salt of the earth God's people are called to be. When our cities and nations are weighed on the scales of Heaven, a handful of these precious consecrated ones can tip the balance in favor of revival rather than destruction.

God is issuing a wake-up call to the Church. If our cities and our nation are to be saved from the coming devastation, we must rise as intercessors before the throne and perform the priestly function found in Joel chapter 2—weeping over America, confessing her sins, and again beseeching the Lord to stay His hand of judgment—*as even the child in Ray Clarke's dream did.*

> *Let the priests, who minister before the Lord, weep between the temple porch and the altar. Let them say, "Spare Your people, O Lord. Do not make Your inheritance an object of scorn, a byword among the nations. Why should they say among the peoples, 'Where is their God?'"* (Joel 2:17)

There is no other way to experience the blessings of restoration and revival that are our promised inheritance. As Mario Murillo so astutely declares, "Before a great awakening, there must come a rude awakening."[11]

Jubilee or judgment—which will it be? The Jewish year of Jubilee was not only about rejoicing; it was also about consecration. The blowing of the ram's horn—or *shofar*—in ancient Israel to begin Jubilee did more than announce the forgiveness of debt and the freedom from bondage for enslaved Jews. The sound of the *shofar* in Jubilee fell on the Day of Atonement and was also a national call to repentance.[12]

In this season of Jubilees that America is now experiencing, the Lord is again calling His people to national repentance. The swiftness with which we respond to this summons and the depth of our repentance and consecration will determine to a large extent whether the hand of the Lord visits America with judgment or blessing.

There can be no doubt that around the world, this century has seen the most dramatic and extensive outpourings of the Holy Spirit that history has ever known. May we be such a people that the close of our century sees the same gracious outpouring from the Lord as in the beginning of the century, when the Azusa Street Revival, the birth of Pentecostalism, changed history forever.

May we postpone judgment and the severest destruction of America by the tears of our repentance, the groanings of our intercession, and the redigging of the historic wells of revival. Then may the latter glory be greater than the former as the wondrous presence of the Lord fills our land with a Jubilee like the world has yet to see!

Chapter 2

There's a Well Beneath Your Feet — Dig It!

A Macedonian Call

On April 29, 1992, I watched with millions of other viewers as Los Angeles was scorched and shamed by the riots that followed the acquittal of the police officers charged in the beating of Rodney King. For eight years we had labored, crying out to God, "Pasadena for God!" I will never forget weeping and interceding before the television as I watched Reginald Denny and others being beaten as whole city blocks blazed out of control. Where was the mighty revival our city had been promised?

Two days later, our pastoral team joined with other concerned pastors from the Los Angeles area in an emergency prayer session. Jack Hayford led our time together. As we interceded for our city, a large African-American pastor stood and began to pour out his pain. As he prayed and cried out for Los Angeles, I looked over at Ché Ahn, my senior pastor. He was weeping uncontrollably. It seemed as if waves of brokenness were rolling over him.

Ché and I have been close friends for many years. In 1982, he received a dream from the Lord that has shaped his destiny and that of many others. In an experience very similar to Paul's Macedonian call, a large black man appeared before Ché, motioning urgently toward him. He said, "Come to Los Angeles. There's going to be a great harvest!" Under the immediacy of the presence of the Holy Spirit, Ché awoke trembling, with this song in his spirit,

> *Go forth, go forth into the reapers' fields,*
> *for they are white unto harvest.*
> *The time, the time of reaping is at hand*
> *for the harvest of the souls of men to be gathered in.*
> *What was sown in tears shall now be reaped with joy....*
> *In the power of the Spirit, revival begins.*

Two years later, with the blessing of other Church leaders, Ché began to form a ministry team to go West. Having grown up in Southern California, I sensed that God was also leading me to Los Angeles. In 1984, 12 of us left Maryland to plant a church in the "Crown City" of Pasadena, just minutes away from downtown Los Angeles.

As I watched Ché weep at the meeting of intercession in 1992, I could only wonder what was going on in his heart. Later, Ché told me excitedly, "Lou, that black pastor who was praying was the same man I saw in my dream in 1982! After the meeting, I had gone to the man and asked, 'Have you been praying long for Los Angeles?' He replied that he had been interceding for Los Angeles since 1982, the very year that I had my dream!"

I was stunned and shocked by Ché's words. I was also bursting with hope. Despite the rubble of the riots, God was giving us a sign that His covenant promises would not fail and there is still hope for our city. I believe that the Lord still remembers another black man who prayed for revival in Los Angeles decades ago. His name was William Seymour.

In 1905, as a black Holiness pastor, William Seymour studied under Charles Parham in Houston, Texas. Because of segregation laws, he was prohibited from joining the classes, so he sat outside the building and listened through the door. Shortly thereafter, a small Holiness church in Los Angeles asked Seymour to preach, with the possibility that he would be invited to become their pastor. When Seymour preached on the baptism of the Holy Spirit with the evidence of speaking in tongues, he was immediately locked out of the church. But God would have the last word in allowing Seymour to change history.

Seymour was then invited to start holding meetings in a home at 216 Bonnie Brae Street, in the downtown Los Angeles area. There an earnest band of saints tarried and fasted for ten days, after which the promised Pentecostal explosion came suddenly out of Heaven. From the innermost part of their beings burst forth rivers of living water that would become known as the Azusa Street Revival, the greatest Pentecostal well in recent history. Thousands from around the world came to drink from this mighty Holy Spirit well that William Seymour and those he met with on Bonnie Brae Street opened in Los Angeles. In 1992, nearly 90 years after that artesian well of revival was opened by William Seymour and the saints who tarried with him, Ché Ahn and another black man named Roosevelt found themselves, like Isaac of old, to be digging the wells of their fathers.[1]

A Dream of Destiny

My own experience has been very much like Ché's. In 1986 I felt drawn to reread *Azusa Street*, a book by Frank Bartleman that I had previously read. Bartleman was a man whose heart burned and thirsted for revival. In 1904, after hearing F.B. Myers describe the great Welsh Revival where not just individuals but entire cities were succumbing to the Lord, Bartleman longed for the same thing to happen in Los Angeles. At the time, his little three-year-old daughter, Esther, had just died. Despite his broken heart, Bartleman gave up his job and dedicated himself to see revival come. During this time, he wrote hundreds of pamphlets and tracts, which he distributed wherever he could. So greatly did the desire for revival consume

Bartleman that his whole life became one of praying and of exhorting the saints to believe for revival. At one point, his wife even feared for his life because he so intensely fasted and prayed. Concerning this, Bartleman wrote,

"My health is quite poor, but I believe I shall live to finish my work. Few care to go into the hard places, but my work is to go where others will not go. It seems God can only get a man who has nothing but Heaven to live for to do the work for which a strong man is needed. I am glad to be used up in His service. I would rather wear out than rust out; and rather starve for God, if need be, than fatten for the devil."[2]

Then in 1906 the floodgates of Heaven opened. Bartleman would later join with those who gathered in the small home on Bonnie Brae Street where a "second Pentecost" fell on the tiny prayer meeting led by William Seymour.

As I reread *Azusa Street* in 1986, I entered an extended period of fasting and prayer. So strongly did God's burden for revival come upon me that I began to cry out, "Give me the mantle of Frank Bartleman! Give me revival like they saw in 1906 at Azusa Street. I want to pray like this man!" Late into the night I called on God. It was as if every fiber of my being was reaching out for the spiritual inheritance that Frank Bartleman had opened in Los Angeles nearly a century before. Like Elisha, who wasn't going to leave Elijah until he had received his mantle,[3] I recognized that I was heir to the same spiritual DNA as this Pentecostal pioneer. In truth, a transference occurred that night. As I cried out in prayer, I was being led to redig the well of my forefather, Frank Bartleman. When the burden lifted, I went to bed.

The next day, Chris Berglund, a prophetic brother and covenant friend for whom I have the deepest affection, shared a dream with me, which he had had the night before. Knowing nothing of what I had prayed, Chris told me, "I saw a large black book, and on the front of the cover in white letters was the title, 'REVIVAL.' When I turned to the inside of the cover, I saw a man's face. The name of the man was Frank Bartleman. As I was looking at his face, the picture suddenly turned into your face, Lou! I closed the book and said, 'I must get this book to Lou!' "

I was astonished by this revelation, accepting Chris' dream as the word of the Lord for me. I knew that it was nothing less than a Joseph-type dream, a dream that God had graciously given to confirm that He had heard my prayers and that He would allow me to be part of a great revival that would come to Pasadena and Los Angeles.

This covenant dream, and the faithful God who gave it, have been an anchor through many difficult seasons. Even now this dream stirs me to believe for wonderful things to come. As if Chris' dream was not enough encouragement, a few weeks later I met a black lady named Dorothy Evans. She knew nothing of me and my Bartleman dream but told me, "In 1906, there was a black lady praying for revival with Frank Bartleman. I feel like I'm that lady and I'm looking for my Bartleman!" She and several other women had been praying and fasting for seven days and nights, camping out in sleeping bags at her church and tenaciously imploring God to bring revival to Pasadena. She was redigging ancient wells.

I believe that in some measure, the mantle of Frank Bartleman was thrown upon me that night in 1986, and our hearts were joined in the cause. I knew that I had tapped into the underground waters of revival flowing beneath this city. I felt like Isaac, returning to the places where his father had lived and drinking from the same wells that he had dug.

There is a river whose streams make glad the city of God, the holy place where the Most High dwells (Psalm 46:4).

There is such incredible spiritual and natural significance in the understanding of wells and water in the Bible. Jesus Himself used the analogy of living water to describe the inestimable value of His life inside us when we tap our own "well" of the Holy

Spirit. But perhaps in stories like Isaac's in the Old Testament, we find the clearest definition of the value of a well.

Rediscovering Ancient Sources of Anointing

Like his nomadic father, Isaac moved his herds around, seeking pasture. When a time of famine drove him northwest, retracing Abraham's steps from Beer Lahai Roi to Gerar, in Philistine territory, Isaac searched for the wells his father had dug so many years before.

Wells and water were the most important consideration for life in that day. They were the source of life and the determining factor for where and how any life could be sustained, any home could be chosen, or any city could be birthed. A good well could last several thousand years and refresh many generations. Jacob's well was a good example of such a lasting patriarchal source of blessing, still providing water to the Samaritans of Jesus' day!

Isaac found that the wells of his father had been rendered useless because the Philistines had filled them in with dirt and stones. So he chose to *redig* the wells of his father:

Isaac reopened the wells that had been dug in the time of his father Abraham, which the Philistines had stopped up after Abraham died, and he gave them the same names his father had given them (Genesis 26:18).

Redigging Abraham's wells was a wise decision. Because of the great difficulty of digging and the expense in time and manpower, it was preferable to redig a previous well than to start anew. In fact, pre-existing wells were so valuable that rival tribes would rather fight over an old well than dig a new one!

Yet even digging an old well anew is a lengthy, laborious, and frequently unpleasant task. Revivalist Tommy Tenney tells this story about one well redug:

"When a friend of mine bought some property in India, he found old machinery, discarded furniture, trash, weeds, bushes, and nearly *300 cobras* when he cleared out an abandoned well that had been dug horizontally into the side of a mountain. What a monumental job! However, the work proved to be worth the effort. The morning after the well was completely cleared, he awoke to find a stream bubbling forth and flowing again."[4]

Revival Wells

I believe God is saying we can go to the wells of our spiritual forefathers and dig again to find new streams of revival bubbling forth. I am not speaking of redigging a well to return to the traditions of the past, or to rediscover old methods or cherished doctrine. Rather I am talking of coming alive again with the waters of the Holy Spirit that were found in the wells of our spiritual ancestors!

I am convinced that such a thing has happened in Pensacola, Florida. Six years before this revival well began to flow again, God spoke to Renée DeLoriea in a Kansas airport, telling her of the revival that would come, which would be a rebirth of a previous well:

"...people were looking at me strangely, but I knew the force backing me into that wall was the power of God. I had been walking down the corridor, minding my own business, when an incredible force pushed me backward... My muscles fell limp like spaghetti, and when I finally hit the wall, I felt almost weightless. I tried to brace myself by leaning on the wall for support, but again the same powerful force began pushing me sideways to the floor. I thought, *Oh great, I bet those people are **really** looking now.* As I was pushed farther and farther to the floor, God spoke to my spirit in an almost audible voice, clearly saying, '*Azusa Street*: Pensacola, Florida. *Azusa Street*: Pensacola, Florida.'

"That day in January, 1989, I knew that God was going to send a revival to Pensacola, Florida. I realized even then that this revival would somehow touch the world just as the

Azusa Street Revival in Los Angeles had changed the course of Church history in the early 1900's."[5]

In a smaller way, God has reopened a revival well at Mott Auditorium, the home of Harvest Rock Church, where I am based in Pasadena, California. On January 1, 1995, while many folks were enjoying the famous Rose Parade held annually in Pasadena on New Year's Day, more than 2,000 believers from all around Los Angeles gathered in Mott Auditorium on short notice to hear John Arnott from the Toronto Airport Christian Fellowship—another renewed well of revival—speak.

The sense of the Lord's presence was tangible, and the shouting and groaning of the saints resounded through the great hall. Many people shook violently and fell to the ground as the Lord came in power. Lives were being transformed and nobody wanted to go home. (The meetings went way beyond midnight.) Some people were saved; others were instantly healed. One lady, Joy Rittenhouse, had suffered six years from severe back pain. During worship that night, she began repeating, "I renounce bitterness. I renounce bitterness." Then it happened. The back pain just disappeared and the precious woman was healed of both inner and outer suffering. On the ministry floor afterward, an unseen power struck her backward, without anyone praying for her. Then a great joy rolled up from within her and she began to laugh uncontrollably. God was turning her mourning into joy. It was Jubilee![6]

This same kind of story can be told by hundreds, if not thousands, who have come to Mott Auditorium and have been personally touched and refreshed by the Lord. Since that New Year's Day when the Holy Spirit's power and presence began to reside in Mott Auditorium and to flow in a demonstrative way, thousands from all over the world have come here to drink of the Holy Spirit. Three years after the initial outpouring of God's Spirit, we are still holding protracted meetings, and a whole new fellowship of churches, called Harvest International Ministries, has been birthed. Many times when the presence of God comes, the sweet rose fragrance of Jesus can be smelled throughout the auditorium. Oh, the beauty of Jesus, the glory of His presence! I believe that Frank Bartleman's wells are being opened again here.

The beauty of Jesus and the presence and power of the Holy Spirit are evident in a demonstrative way wherever God opens a well of revival. There is a "glory" that rests on both the place and the people. Those who come, drink deeply.

Yet not all revival wells flow in the same way. Toronto, Canada, for example, is a well of refreshing. Pensacola, on the other hand, is a well of salvation. Despite this variation in the way revival wells flow, a consistent series of results accompanies the opening of every well.

First, a revival well provides water that refreshes and revives dying people who are spiritually thirsty. When Hagar fled into the desert of Beersheba, she cried out to God for water to give to her son Ishmael, who was all but dead. God mercifully responded by opening her eyes so that she could see a well of fresh water.[7] That drink in the desert saved her life and the life of her son. How many thousands, or *millions,* are dying in our cities—just looking for a well of revival?

Second, revival wells are communal in nature. All are free to come and receive of the well's refreshing. This is part of the beauty of revival. Believers from every race and denomination come together and stand side by side at the same pool. Maintaining this communal nature requires a soft spirit of all who would drink the well's refreshing waters.

When Ché and I went to Toronto in October of 1994, we found ourselves face to face with brothers from the denomination we had just left. In fact, you just might find yourself worshiping with the person who split your church fellowship six months before! At this point, each seeker must choose whether to bless his or her brothers and sisters in the Lord or to dispute them at the well.

Disputes at the well are nothing new. When Isaac became so wealthy that he threatened the surrounding Philistines, they forced him out and his servants had to dig new wells. So Isaac's men dug two new wells, which the shepherds of Gerar claimed, again forcing Isaac to move on. Isaac named the first abandoned well *Esek*, which means "quarreling." He named the second *Sitnah*, which means "accusation." Only after they dug the third well were Isaac, his family, and his servants left in peace. This well Isaac named *Rehoboth*, meaning "open place" or "room for all."[8]

When strife and bickering over the use of a well erupts, be it a physical well or a spiritual one, the entire community suffers. Everyone misses the blessing it might provide. Then what was meant to be a place of refreshing for all people (like the disputed wells Isaac was forced to leave) becomes a perpetual reminder of ugly disagreements and soul-wrenching disputes. History confirms that all attempts to control a well in the Spirit always end up stopping the flow. Bitterness, selfish ambition, fear, resentment, pride, deception…whatever the source of the conflict or division, dissension has always resulted in the loss of the water both sides were trying to safeguard. Then the glory of revival is forgotten and only the memory of the differences and divisions remains. We must not forget that the water found at revival wells is given by God for the refreshing and blessing of all!

Third, the water from a true revival well is transferable. That is, it can be taken home, thereby impacting many people who may not have the opportunity to go to the well and get a drink. The water from Toronto and Pensacola, for example, has touched the lives of multitudes of people who have never traveled to either city. There is a tangible presence of God that goes with it that can be shared with others.

Ché Ahn and I intentionally went to the Anaheim Vineyard Conference in 1994, where a well was flowing, so that we could receive some of the fresh water. We received the blessing of the Spirit. Soon afterward, we planted Harvest Rock Church, and that same power and blessing began to fall on our people. It was definitely transferable!

Fourth, wonderful ministries that bless thousands of people begin to form around a revival well. Bible schools and training centers are established, ministries to the poor are released, and missionary vision explodes. In my home church in Pasadena alone, four other churches have merged with us to form Harvest Rock Church. Anointed men, and my treasured friends, Rick Wright, Karl Malouff, Jim Johnston, and Carlos Quintero, all laid down their senior pastor positions for the greater vision. Now, from this one church blended from five congregations, we are starting a school of ministry for church planters and missionaries and a food bank for ministry to the poor. We also support an international ministry that sends out apostolic men to train and encourage the more than 180 related churches that have already joined our Harvest International Ministries. All this began because one well broke open! I believe this happens because wells, by their very nature, tap into a hidden source of water that provides continual refreshing. Revival wells, in particular, sustain a fresh relationship with the Lord that empowers those who drink from it.

Dig Wells—Not Cisterns!

The temptation that confronts all who find refreshing at revival wells is to stop relying on the Lord and to start depending on themselves. In a heartbroken cry, the Lord rebuked Israel for this sin: "My people have committed two sins: They have forsaken Me, the spring of living water, and have dug their own cisterns, broken cisterns that cannot hold water" (Jer. 2:13). This lament starts with the Lord's fond memory of Israel: "I remember the devotion of your youth, how as a bride you loved Me..." (Jer. 2:2).

Forsaking the Lord and digging our own cisterns is losing the freshness of our early affection for the Lord and finding other things to satisfy us. It is doing the very thing that Paul warned the

Galatians against: "…After beginning with the Spirit, are you now trying to attain your goal by human effort?" (Gal. 3:3)

Cisterns, by their very nature, cannot supply the fresh, living (flowing) water found in natural springs or wells. This is true because wells are supplied by fresh underground water, whereas cisterns are but small reservoirs dug in the ground to collect and store rainwater. Water is channeled into the cisterns by drains from roofs, courtyards, streets, and in some places, open areas of land. Therefore, debris and filth collect in the tank along with the water. This sediment eventually settles to the bottom of the reservoir, oftentimes polluting the water.

How often has the Church sought to hollow out a little tank outside the back door, wanting to store up every drop of rain that might fall her way? How often have we resorted to religious control as we've tried to contain what little life there is in our churches, frantically plastering away at every crack in our facade, as the owner of a cistern might plaster the cracks in the rock to prevent the water from escaping? Like the manna that was to be eaten fresh every day except on the Sabbath,[9] the refreshing water of the Spirit must be received fresh and new each day.

The Process of Digging

We at Harvest Rock Church have learned that if water is to last more than a few brief weeks, we cannot be satisfied to stop digging when we're wading in ankle-deep water. We must dig to depths that provide a steady, life-sustaining flow. This has required much perseverance because digging after we found water was not easy. In fact, the deeper we dug, the harder it became. Let me share with you a few insights we have gained about how to dig a well of revival and what happens while you are digging.

First, you'll probably be thirsty while you are digging. To dig or redig a well is hard work. You may feel that your efforts are feeble (and ours have been!), but no rock can withstand a constant tapping or hammering on the same spot without cracking.

Keep on praying! God, in His mercy, gives an intense spiritual thirst during this season that keeps you desperate for His presence. It is this thirst that keeps you digging.

Second, the Lord will give you a prophetic surge every now and then to encourage you. This may be in the form of words, dreams, or divine appointments or coincidences. Hold on to these revelations dearly, for they will propel you when you see no water!

Third, expect demonic resistance and push through discouragement and dryness. Very often the enemy tries to hinder access to life-giving wells. Even as intercessors have contended and continue to contend for the spiritual "gates," so you must fight for your spiritual wells of refreshing. Gather a company of committed prayer warriors who are not intimidated by the enemy. They must be people like the mighty men of David's band, who braved great danger to satisfy David's desire for a drink from the well at Bethlehem when he was separated from it by Philistine forces:

So the three mighty men broke through the Philistine lines, drew water from the well near the gate of Bethlehem and carried it back to David....Such were the exploits of the three mighty men (2 Samuel 23:16-17).

Fourth, learn to worship. As you get closer to water, worship becomes a major emphasis. It is worship and praise that opens the fountains in the desert, and water from the rock: "Spring up, O well; sing ye into it" (Num. 21:17b KJV).

Fifth, don't give up once you've hit water. Many people make the mistake of backing off when God finally releases His refreshing Spirit. This is precisely the time to press forward for greater victory. When John Arnott, the pastor of Airport Christian Fellowship in Toronto, saw the moving of the Holy Spirit during those first few meetings with Randy Clark, he was not content to have just some good meetings. He wanted more, so he asked Randy to stay on longer. He held protracted meetings. This strategy of holding protracted meetings is the first counsel that Wes Campbell gave to us when the Spirit began to move in Mott Auditorium. It is counsel that you, too, must heed if you would open and sustain the flow of the Holy Spirit from the wells beneath your feet.

Many ancient wells descended to great depths. (Jacob's well is still 75 feet deep, having been at least twice that deep at one time.) This was necessary because shallow wells often ran dry in the heat of summer. The same is true for wells of revival. Satan will try many things to prevent you from digging deep wells. Should this fail, he'll send opposition your way or he'll try to provoke you into putting limits on what God's Spirit may do and how He may do it. When you do strike water—make sure to stay in it!

This may sound obvious, but many churches miss the full blessing by backing off after a few meetings in the power of renewal and revival. They go back to church "the way it was" and figure that the evident outpouring of God's Spirit was a passing thing. Keep praying and inviting the Holy Spirit. Contend for your inheritance!

The wells that Frank Bartleman and others dug were wells of deep devotion. They were wells from which living water flowed through a fresh, vital relationship with the Lord Jesus Christ. In time, however, those wells of refreshing became stopped up by stones of contention, division, and institutionalism. Those who had drunk deeply from their waters began to rely more on cisterns, which are the idolatry and religious activity that characterize much of the Church today.

In biblical times, old cisterns were often used as prisons. At least two prophets, Joseph and Jeremiah, were imprisoned in them! Dead bodies were also thrown into these unused pits.[10] This sounds a lot like what Jesus condemned the Pharisees for:

Woe to you, teachers of the law and Pharisees, you hypocrites! You are like whitewashed tombs, which look beautiful on the outside but on the inside are full of dead men's bones and everything unclean (Matthew 23:27).

If we want to see sustained "watering holes" open across our land, we must keep digging, not build storage tanks! Religious cisterns, like physical cisterns, cannot provide fresh water. Although the building of religious cisterns may appear to be an attempt to preserve the move of God we are enjoying, in truth such efforts result only in the neglect of the very wells from which the refreshing waters flow. Then those places that were once sources of life become places of death instead.

An article in the *Los Angeles Times* illustrates this principle all too well. The article told the story of a five-year-old boy in Buenos Aires, Argentina, who fell down a 59-foot well shaft while he was out walking with his mother. The well, located in the middle of a grassy field, had been dug four years earlier; but it had been neglected and had become overgrown with weeds. Hidden as it was by the weeds, it became a death trap for this young child. Only when she heard his shout did the mother realize that her son, who had been walking behind her, had fallen into the abandoned well. Rescuers had to dig a parallel tunnel so that they could reach the trapped child. After spending more than 33 hours in the well, the child was pulled out, but doctors were unable to revive him.

What struck me about this story was the young boy's name: Cristian.[11] His story broke my heart when I read it. The well that had been dug to be a source of blessing and refreshing ended up being a trap of death.

Many revival wells have suffered this fate. They have become places of death where the life-giving water that once bubbled up to revive and nourish all who drank it now flows silently, unnoticed and untapped. These are the wells that you and I are called to clear out and reopen.

It's time to reclaim the lost promises and unfulfilled potential of the many revival wells that have been dug throughout the history of the Church. God is seeking to restore our rightful inheritance. So before you begin digging a new well, try to reopen an old well by researching and reclaiming the history of revival in your area. Discover what "springs of water welling up to eternal life"[12] are part of the heritage of your family and of the congregation and denomination into which the Lord has planted you. As John Dawson writes,

> "Do not despise your roots. Every Israelite had a tribe. There were no independent Jews. Sectarian attitudes are wrong, but denominations are biblical. God sets us in families in His kingdom. If you do not know your inheritance, how can you enter into it? How can you rejoice in it?"[13]

Many denominations were birthed in revival! It's time that we rediscover the ancient inheritances upon which the Church has been founded. It's time to clear out the original wells of revival that have been polluted by division and the traditions of man. This is the season when sons and daughters can repossess the wells that their fathers and mothers fought to dig. May we by our repentance, forgiveness, and prayer, restore the effervescent flow of the Holy Spirit that has long been stopped up and forgotten. May we reclaim and rename the revival wells that now only recall disputes and disagreement, and instead honor the memory of those who originally established these historic sources of life-giving water.

The glory of God that bubbled up and spilled over in days past will again arise to refresh God's people and to bless them with a presence and power of God's Spirit that many have only read about and longed for. Then the life-giving wells dug by Frank Bartleman and other saints throughout the ages will flow freely, testifying to the faithfulness and covenant-keeping nature of God. Men and women will again wear the mantles of saints who fasted, prayed, and tarried until the glory of God came down. There's a well beneath your feet. Dig it, lest you die!

Chapter 3

Restoring the Hearts of the Fathers to Their Children

A Multigenerational Blessing: The Spark for Revival

In early 1997, I went to preach to a church in Lake Isabella, California. I had told no one about the theme of my message: *You are the great-grandchildren of Jonathan Edwards. Therefore God will pour out His Spirit upon you.* Minutes before the meeting began, a young man I did not know came up to me and excitedly exclaimed, "Mr. Engle, I just found out that I'm the great-great-great-great-grandson of Jonathan Edwards." Stunned, I replied, "You've got to be kidding me!" At that moment the Holy Spirit said to me,

> *"Lou, you are on target. I'm going to keep My covenant with America. I'm going to raise up a covenantal generation who will fast and pray, who will be rebuilders of the breach and turn the tide again."*

My heart exploded, and I knew that I was on to something.

God had been putting such a hunger in me to ignite people's passion to discover their spiritual genealogy and heritage and to receive a spiritual inheritance and identity from those great forefathers and mothers who went before us. Now another piece of the puzzle was also coming into view. I had been reading *Feast of Fire* by John Kilpatrick, pastor of the Brownsville Assembly of God Church in Pensacola, Florida. Something about that particular revival struck me. God kept impressing upon me that the Pensacola revival is a special sign of how He wants to bring forth outpourings in these last days. I began to see it as a picture of what could happen when the hearts of the fathers are turned to the children, and the hearts of the children to the fathers.

I've heard people say that John Kilpatrick and Stephen Hill, the pastor and evangelist at Pensacola, must be more holy than most Christians for the fire to fall in Pensacola. Without a doubt, these men walk closely with God in brokenness, prayer, and obedience, but there is much more at work in Pensacola than the godliness of these two men. God is keeping His covenant with a pastor, a spiritual father who labored among the teenage boys of the area in days past.

John Kilpatrick's father left his family when John was only 12 years old. At age 14, John received a powerful call to the ministry, at which time Pastor R.C. Wetzel approached John's mother about discipling her son. With his mother's permission, John became one of a group of teenage boys that Pastor Wetzel gathered together each week. These boys felt called to the ministry. Pastor Wetzel would teach them the Scriptures then have each one, in turn, teach the others what they had learned. For two years these kids joined Pastor Wetzel for daily midnight prayer meetings. Thus this pastor fathered the fatherless John Kilpatrick.

One night the Holy Spirit fell. Brother Wetzel later told the kids that the Lord had spoken to him that night, telling him to stay on in Pensacola and multiply himself in these teenage boys. "If you do that," God told him, "you will reach more people through these young preachers than you could ever reach on your own."[1] For the next many years, Pastor Wetzel poured his life into John Kilpatrick and the others. The old man died never having seen the prophecy fulfilled.

As I read this account in John Kilpatrick's book, I was deeply moved. Pastor Wetzel was a real father. He was more concerned about the next generation than about his own ministry. He offered up his Isaac, and like Abraham, was promised offspring beyond number. Then I saw it! The Spirit of God fell in Pensacola on *Father's Day*, 1995! God was saying, "It's Father's Day! I can't contain Myself!" So with Pastor Wetzel and the great cloud of witnesses gazing down, God sent fire on the old pastor's offering.

The current fires of revival and renewal are not so much about Stephen Hill and John Kilpatrick, or about Lou Engle or John Arnott, but about Leonard Ravenhill, Pastor Wetzel, Jacob Engle, and John Wimber. We must understand with humility that we stand on the shoulders of many great men and women of God who have gone before us. We must give honor where honor is due. The Holy Spirit's outpouring in these last days of the twentieth century is founded in father-son and mother-daughter connections. God is establishing the work of today's intercessors on the foundation of those godly men and women who prayed down His glory in days gone by.

Every altar, every revival well in history, will be restored because God is a covenant-keeping God. Once He has spoken, His promises cannot be revoked; He cannot lie. In truth, He will fulfill every word He speaks. Some generation will receive the covenantal promise as God intended and will arise and inherit all that was promised!

Think of the crisis in the youth of our nation alone—and how their heart cry is for identity. What would happen if our kids could tap into the reality of the great spiritual heritage to which God has called them? Some say, "The past is past, and

God is doing a new thing. Just move forward and forget about the old." But this wrongly interprets the heart of a God who keeps His covenant to generations! As John Dawson writes of his own country, Britain:

> "The vacant-eyed punkers and young urban professionals of British cities are the great-grandchildren of Livingstone, Wesley, Whitefield, Booth, Wycliffe, Fox, Studd and Taylor. The lives of these great heroes of the faith were intercessory acts. Their prayers still ascend before the throne of God. When God weighs Britain in the balance, the scales are heavy with missionary martyrs who gave their lives in Africa and China."[2]

God will not forget! He will visit the natural and spiritual children of these heroes of the faith!

Returning to Spiritual Forefathers

Early in 1997, I was invited to a renewal tent meeting in San Pedro, California. Although there was only a handful of people in attendance, the presence of the Lord was so real and my spirit became alive in a new way. As I stood in that meeting, a drop of water fell from the top of the tent and hit me on the forehead. It felt to me as if it was one of the tears of Heaven. Suddenly my heart was opened wide and the Holy Spirit spoke to me quite clearly,

> *"In the last days, because I said in My Word that I will pour out the spirit of Elijah in the last days, I will reopen every well of revival dug by the forefathers and foremothers of faith. And I will restore the hearts of the fathers to their children, and the hearts of the children to their fathers. As it was in the days of Noah, the fountains of the deep will be opened up and the floodgates of the heavens will be opened. As surely as I live, all the earth will be filled with the glory of the Lord."*

I was stunned by this prophetic word that flowed from me. For the next few hours, I preached on the redigging of the wells of the Moravians, the Nazarenes, the Pentecostals, and the Jesus Movement.

> *See, I will send you the prophet Elijah before that great and dreadful day of the Lord comes. He will turn the hearts of the fathers to their children, and the hearts of the children to their fathers; or else I will come and strike the land with a curse* (Malachi 4:5-6).

There are two turnings talked about here: fathers to the children, and children to the fathers. For years I have understood this passage to mean that God was going to bring a move of the spirit of Elijah to heal individual family relationships in the last days. Without a doubt, this is part of the truth contained in this Scripture, but there is much more. As C.F. Keil writes,

> "The meaning of this [Malachi 4:5-6] is not that he will settle disputes in families, or restore peace between parents and children; for the leading sin of the nation at the time of our prophet was not family quarrels, but estrangement from God. The fathers are rather the ancestors of the Israelitish nation, the patriarchs, and generally the pious forefathers, such as David... The sons or children are the degenerate descendants of Malachi's own time and the succeeding ages."[3]

This Scripture is not primarily about bringing dads together with their kids; it is about a whole generation returning to the God of their fathers—that is, getting back to the hearts of their spiritual forefathers.

During the epic battle between Yahweh and Baal on Mt. Carmel, Elijah prayed a generation-restoring prayer of the kind that Malachi speaks of:

> *O Lord, God of Abraham, Isaac and Israel, let it be known today that You are God in Israel.... Answer me, O Lord, answer me, so these people will know that You, O Lord, are God, and that You are turning their hearts back again* (1 Kings 18:36b-37).

John the Baptist embodied this same spirit. He received the mantle that had been on Elijah hundreds of years before. Like Elijah, he called a whole nation to repent and turn back to the God of their fathers.

Turning the heart of the fathers to the sons does not mean merely directing the love of the fathers *to* the sons, but also restoring the heart of the fathers *in* the sons. It is not about returning to their methodology, but to their hearts, their passions, and their sacrifice. Sons receive their forefathers' disposition and affections and are prompted to renew the covenants that had been made between God and their ancestors.

This renewing of covenant is founded upon repentance and surrender to the new work of God within. Apart from repentance, there can be no restoration and no inheritance of God's promises. John the Baptist's scathing rebuke of the Pharisees points to the deadliness of returning or clinging to our heritage without the necessary change of heart:

> *You brood of vipers! Who warned you to flee from the coming wrath? Produce fruit in keeping with repentance. And do not think you can say to yourselves, "We have Abraham as our father." I tell you that out of these stones God can raise up children for Abraham* (Matthew 3:7b-9).

The Pharisees trusted in their past but lacked power in the present. Theirs was a self-satisfied pride that stirred nationalistic zeal, relying on the greatness of their ancestry to spare them from judgment. Their boastful confidence was a far cry from the humble repentance and faith that had characterized the very ancestors on whom the Pharisees founded their pride. John, like Elijah before him, called his people to a heart relationship with their God, not to a relationship based solely on genealogical ties. It wasn't enough to recite the glorious history of God's dealings with Israel in the past. John sought to arouse the hearts of Abraham's children to renew the covenant made between Yahweh and Abraham.

Our country is in need of the same reconditioning of heart that the people of Elijah's day and the generation of John the Baptist needed. Just being part of a denomination with a glorious past is not enough. Neither will reciting the history of revival prepare the way for the Lord to visit us as He fell upon our forefathers. True sons and daughters have their parents' spiritual affections.

Malachi also writes of a second breach that must be healed: Not only must the hearts of the children be turned, but also the hearts of the fathers. The sad history of revival has been that the leaders used in one outpouring of God's Spirit have not recognized the next move of God when it came.

The Foursquare Church founded by Aimee Semple McPherson has been the root of many blessings in Los Angeles, each with its own gifting and strength. Chuck Smith, founder of Calvary Chapel, came out of the Foursquare movement. Begun with powerful demonstrations of the Holy Spirit during the Jesus Movement, Calvary Chapel has carried a great mandate for evangelism and discipleship. John Wimber, a son of Calvary Chapel, was used powerfully to start Vineyard Fellowship, which has blessed the whole Body of Christ with the gift of worship and the vision of equipping the saints to minister. The Vineyard, in turn, has birthed many of the renewal churches of the late 1990's in which thousands have been restored, refreshed, and empowered for service. At each birth, there have been misunderstandings and wounds between the fathers and the sons.

The cry of my heart is that the Church will both redig the wells of revival dug by our spiritual ancestors and release the children of revival to move on into new dimensions of experiencing and serving God. This rebuilding of covenant between God and America is not a dream. It's a valid potential in the heart of God. He's looking for believers who will turn their hearts to their spiritual forefathers, and for fathers of revival and renewal who will turn their hearts to their children. He's raising up a people who will say, "I will fulfill the divine requirements for such a move as this."

Spiritual Amnesia

At an airport one day, I began talking about the Lord with a woman who was waiting for her flight. When I asked her what denomination she was part of, she replied, "The Foursquare." "Oh," I said, "Aimee Semple McPherson was awesome." I was totally surprised and disappointed when she replied, "Oh, our church is trying to distance ourselves from that Pentecostal stuff." In my heart, I was saying, "That Pentecostal stuff shook the nations. I've read your history! And I know that even now there are Foursquare pastors who are reclaiming this heritage."

At Angeles Temple, where Aimee Semple McPherson ministered, thousands of people were saved and healed of every kind of sickness and disease. The casts and braces still on display there testify to the gracious outpouring of God's Spirit that occurred within those walls. This outpouring shook Los Angeles, San Diego, Oakland, Denver, and other cities across America. To be ashamed of that heritage is to fall prey to a dangerous phenomena called *spiritual amnesia*.

Spiritual amnesia happens when a denomination or the offspring of a particular move of the Spirit forgets the fresh revelation of Jesus Christ and the quickening encounter with the Holy Spirit that their forefathers and mothers embraced. The same doctrines are taught, but the power is not present. Whereas apostles first led the way, over time administrators become the leaders. Thus a whole generation arises that has never seen the power that birthed their inheritance.

This truth was affirmed by a Vineyard pastor who spoke at some of our renewal meetings at Mott Auditorium. While he and I were discussing the manifestations of the Spirit that many people were experiencing, he made an interesting comment concerning one denomination that has reacted very negatively about this present wave of revival, "I remember being in that movement in the early days. Hippies and washed out kids attended and worshiped. The power was explosive and the same manifestations of revival were occurring as now. Now they don't remember. They have a case of spiritual amnesia."

Because of this phenomenon, thousands of hungry saints have been locked out of a whole new encounter with the living God. Why? The hearts of the children have not been restored to their fathers; neither have the hearts of the fathers been reconciled to the spiritual children they rejected.

May we and our children be generations who honor and love the spiritual roots from which we have grown, contending for the power of the Holy Spirit, rather than rewriting our history as a bland and powerless but respectable tale. When we are embarrassed by our Pentecostal roots, we become "Punycostals," as my friend Rick Wright says. Even while we confess the sins of our spiritual ancestors and the excesses and imbalances to which they fell prey, may we not neglect or be ashamed of the inheritance they have laid out for us.

Today a clarion call comes to us to "honor our fathers and mothers." The prophetic word of Rick Joyner and others is clear that the promise of stayed destruction is linked to the scriptural command, "Honor your father and your mother, so that you may live long in the land the Lord your God is giving you" (Ex. 20:12). God will postpone judgment if we will simply begin to acknowledge and honor our spiritual progenitors.

The only hope for America in this hour is that God continues to keep His covenant with our forefathers. This does not mean that we can trust in our spiritual inheritance. Rather it demands that we embrace the promises and covenants that are our birthright and appeal in humility before the mercy seat of the God who gave these covenantal promises. In truth, the curse on our nation (and on Los Angeles) will be removed only by a move of God that turns our hearts back to the faith, passion, and power of men and women like Phineas Bresse,[4] William Seymour,[5] Henrietta Mears,[6] Aimee Semple

McPherson,[7] Billy Graham,[8] Bill Bright,[9] Keith Green,[10] Dennis Bennet,[11] and Demos Shakarian.[12]

The prophetic word of our day is sobering and the price we will pay for ignoring it cannot be overestimated. We must arise and redig the wells of our spiritual inheritance, that we, our children, and our children's children may receive the blessings of godly covenants restored. To do otherwise is to face God's judgment on our cities and land.

Chapter 4

Moving the Heart of God Through Sacrifice

Toward the end of 1997, I was experiencing a time of weariness and dryness. Unknown to me, a group of intercessors were praying that the Lord would give my dear friend Chris Berglund a dream for me, to encourage me and launch me into the new year. On the last day of 1997, I received a phone call. It was Chris! He shared with me a powerful prophetic dream that the Lord had just given him.

> "*In the dream, I saw you covered by a cloud like the glory of God. As I was looking down at you, a resounding voice and presence filled the vision. I didn't know if it was the Lord or an angel of the Lord whom I was seeing and hearing, but this Divine Being with a powerful voice started reading Psalm 50 over you. He started with verse 1 and ended with verse 15. I couldn't tell if you were kneeling or standing, but your hands were raised, your tears were flowing, and your head was raised in reverence to this voice, as if to heed every word spoken.*"

In summary, Chris said, "I can best describe the dream as simply 'holy' and very serious. It felt as though the Lord is emphasizing to you that His approval is upon your consecration and your covenant with Him." When Chris shared this dream with an elderly prophetic friend, Bob Lyon, Bob stressed verse 5 of Psalm 50: "Gather to Me My consecrated ones, who have made a covenant with Me by sacrifice." He went on to say, "God has accepted the covenant Lou has made with Him by sacrifice."

This dream has strong implications for me, setting my course in 1998. The significance of this psalm and this prophetic dream is not just for me, however. *Psalm 50 describes God releasing both His covenant judgment and His covenant mercy.* It is no coincidence that the fiftieth psalm is spoken—a reminder that Jubilee or judgment comes in the fiftieth year. I'm so glad that only verses 1 through 15 were read over me in the dream! In these verses, the Lord delivers His godly ones in the midst of trouble. Verse 16 through the end of the psalm speaks of God's terrifying judgment for those who take the covenant upon their lips, but do not obey it. God is coming to judge His people. The crucial question is, Will He find godly ones who have renewed the covenants with Him by sacrifice?

The Lord Does Not Forget Devotion

Covenants in their highest form are strong, irrevocable, and binding commitments forged out of the deep and holy affections between two parties. The expression of affection is through costly sacrifice freely given. A covenant with God guarantees His faithfulness to His promise. Once the covenant is consecrated, God will not, cannot, break it. The covenant is totally binding. The memory of sacrifices of particular devotion are never forgotten, and generations later they still have power to stir the heart of God.

One truly remarkable example of this took place one night in 1983 in a village in Algeria. That night, every inhabitant of the village had a personal, supernatural encounter with God through a combination of dreams, visions, and angelic visitation. Every one of these Muslims received a revelation of Jesus at the same time!

"As the Holy Spirit lingered and these simple citizens managed to piece together the magnitude of what had happened to them, a sense of spiritual awe settled over the entire village. In the weeks that followed, their conclusions led to a dramatic wholesale conversion involving some 400 to 450 Muslim villagers—a nearly eighteen-fold increase in the size of the Algerian national church!

"When amazed mission workers, who had no direct involvement in this extraordinary development, began to investigate possible reasons for this sovereign visitation, they came across a stunning piece of information. It was at virtually this very site that, in June 1315, Raymond Lull, a Spanish missionary from Majorca, had been stoned to death by frenzied Muslims after preaching in the open market.

"The blood of martyrs, it has often been said, represents the seed of the Church. Lull, who is generally considered to be the first missionary to the Muslims, certainly believed this. In his book, *The Tree of Life*, he wrote that Islamic strongholds are best conquered 'by love and prayers, and the pouring out of tears and blood.' In retrospect, it appears that it was precisely this formula that summoned the recent supernatural events in Algeria. Falling into the ground on that summer day in the fourteenth century, the seed of Raymond Lull's poured-out life was subsequently watered by the tears of generations of pious intercessors...

"Adding more luster to this marvelous story is the fact that it has apparently triggered a book of Acts-style revival throughout other parts of Algeria, which continues to this day. During the summer of 1990, I had the privilege of meeting with several dozen former Muslims who had come to faith in Christ within the previous eighteen months. Nearly all reported some type of supernatural intervention. Churches are spreading like wildfire, particularly among the Kabyle Berber people living in and around the Atlas Mountains."[1]

This story contains a picture of Heaven's mercy being poured out on a man's sacrifice. The true nature of revival is God pouring Himself out on someone's sacrifice of love. God always sends fire on the acceptable sacrifice. Whenever the fragrance of obedience born out of love reaches His heart, He erupts with covenant love: "You've given Me your best, now I am bound by love. Here's My best!" This sacrifice birthed from love for God, with the accompanying response of covenant love from God, is clearly revealed in the Scriptures. The story of Abraham and Isaac on Mount Moriah clearly shows us the power of this covenant love.

This is the nature of the relationship between God and Abraham. God has promised to bless Abraham and to make his descendants "too numerous to count" (Gen. 16:10). One day God decides to test His covenant with Abraham, to see whether Abraham will be a faithful covenant partner by surrendering everything to God, as though to say, "What is mine is Yours, and what is Yours is mine." So God says to Abraham, "Take your son, your only son, Isaac, whom you love, and go to the region of Moriah. Sacrifice him there as a burnt offering on one of the mountains I will tell you about" (Gen. 22:2).

Notice this is not a human-initiated sacrifice. God must initiate our sacrifices or they themselves become religious exercises of futility leading to legalism.

Sacrifice and offering You did not desire; my ears You have opened. Burnt offering and sin offering You did not require. Then I said, "Behold, I come; in the scroll of the book it is written of me. I delight to do Your will, O my God, and Your law is within my heart" (Psalm 40:6-8 NKJV).

When God opens our ears, calling for a laying down of an Isaac, He releases grace for it, and our response springs from great desire. Yet it is still a costly sacrifice.

Now remember, Isaac himself was in fact the covenant promise. God had said, "...it is through Isaac that your offspring will be reckoned" (Gen. 21:12). To kill him is to kill the promise. What will Abraham do? Can he make the covenantal transaction God is requiring? Will he love God more than anything, even to the point of giving God his son Isaac—the ultimate sacrifice, the promise itself?

Abraham, because of his Eastern culture, understands covenant. He reasons that God will provide—even if that means raising Isaac from the dead—because God's covenant with him is through Isaac, and God cannot lie. So there on that lonely mountain within the sight of the whole cosmic realm, Abraham prepares to make a covenant by sacrifice.

Tears stream down Abraham's face as he binds Isaac to the altar. The heavens are stunned that Isaac himself, now a strong young man, gives no resistance. Then, as sorrow and love flow mingled down, the knife is lifted, ready to be plunged into the heart of the sacrifice.

Shock waves of astonishment reverberate throughout the ranks of the angelic hosts. They stare in stunned silence. "What kind of love is this?" the angelic tribune wonders. Suddenly the Great Heart of Heaven bursts forth, erupting in heart-rending emotion and commanding the angelic messenger to go with all haste to His covenant friend. With the speed of light, the angel streaks to Moriah and calls, *"Abraham! Abraham!"*

"Here I am," Abraham replies, his spontaneous response springing from the habitual heart response that he has cultivated over many years of loving trust and obedience.

"Do not lay a hand on the boy," he [the angel] *said. "Do not do anything to him. Now I know that you fear God, because you have not withheld from Me your son, your only son"* (Genesis 22:12).

Suddenly it is as if God cannot contain Himself any longer. With deep emotion, He responds to Abraham a second time,

I swear by Myself, declares the Lord, that because you have done this and have not withheld your son, your only son, I will surely bless you and make your descendants as numerous as the stars in the sky and as the sand on the seashore. Your descendants will take possession of the cities of their enemies, and through your offspring all nations on earth will be blessed, because you have obeyed Me (Genesis 22:16-18).

This same response of covenantal love is evident at the cross and the subsequent outpouring of the Holy Spirit on Pentecost. Pentecost cannot be understood only as some divine strategy of Heaven to get out the gospel. Pentecost was the Father's divine eruption on the sacrifice of His "only begotten Son." It is as though God was saying to Jesus, "How can I withhold anything from You? You have paid the ultimate sacrifice." Here is the love gift of My Spirit upon Your Bride."

Suddenly everything changes! God rips open the heavenlies and the atomic power of His love explodes with words that only He could express. Tongues of fire witnessed to the Father's love and approval as He sent fire on the sacrifices of His Son and of His Son's covenant band. In one moment, 3,000 were saved!

Revival—Heaven's Response

Covenant love is what revival is all about. It is not about restoring old practices and methods or reestablishing old traditions. We are seeking to restore the original heart motivations and sacrificial love that moved God to act in revival power in the past. "And he will restore the hearts of the fathers to their children, and the hearts of the children to the fathers" (Mal. 4:6a NAS) is the watchword and promise.

Prior to the Welsh Revival of the early twentieth century, a pastor had told a 13-year-old boy to never miss a prayer meeting because he never would know when the Spirit might fall. That young man, Evan Roberts, prayed for up to 5 nights a week for 13 years. Then in 1904, God erupted in love on the sacrificial prayers of Roberts.[2]

Sacrifice is the key. The power of praying in Jesus' name is that God remembers Jesus' sacrifice and His great heart is moved deeply to respond to us because of it. The power is not primarily in Jesus' intercession for us, but in His willing obedience to suffer death on the cross. Though He cried out to God with loud cries during His days on the earth, He was heard because of His reverent submission.[3] God continues to send His fire on Jesus' sacrifice.

God Revisits the Site of Sacrifice

This remembering of prior acts of sacrifice is what revival is all about. God is a God of personality and passion. A holy nostalgia arises in His heart when He remembers people and places of deep love and sacrifice. This is not unlike the secret longings and memories that arise within us at the sound of a person's name or the name of a certain place.

When I returned to my childhood church, memories of my spiritual experiences in the place where I had met God welled up within me with deep emotion. Here were the places of revival camp meetings where the old brethren would leap for joy and would weep and kiss each other during footwashing and communion services. Here my father wept at the altar. That nostalgia is powerful in moving the heart to act.

The Scriptures seem to indicate that God too has favorite places that He desires to visit because of the offerings of love that were poured out there before Him in the past.

Mount Moriah is certainly one of God's favorite places because of the act of extravagant love Abraham poured out there. Generations later in that same place, King David was the recipient of God's covenantal love and blessing.

Disregarding the law of God, David had numbered the fighting men of Israel. God brought judgment on David's pride.

*So the Lord sent a plague on Israel.... And God sent an
angel to destroy Jerusalem. But as the angel was doing so,
the Lord saw it and was grieved because of the calamity
and said to the angel who was destroying the people,
"Enough! Withdraw your hand." The angel of the Lord
was then standing at the threshing floor of Araunah the
Jebusite* (1 Chronicles 21:14-15).

Why was God so moved in compassion? Certainly His
heart was moved for the people, but might it have been something about the particular spot where the angel stood?

*Then Solomon began to build the temple of the Lord in
Jerusalem on Mount Moriah, where the Lord had
appeared to his father David. It was on the threshing
floor of Araunah the Jebusite, the place provided by
David* (2 Chronicles 3:1).

Mount Moriah and the threshing floor of Araunah were the
same place. The angel of the Lord was passing by the very place
of Abraham's sacrificial obedience. Could it be that God remembered this sacrifice of love, which foreshadowed the sacrifice of
the Lamb of God for the sins of many? Was it as though the
blood of Isaac, yielded up but not shed, cried out from the
ground, "Forgive! Forgive! Forgive!" and the holy offering on
that holy ground moved God to act again in mercy? We cannot
know what entered the heart and mind of God, but we do know
that He stayed the angel's hand when the angel stood at the very
place where Abraham had made the supreme sacrifice.

What must David have felt when he saw the angel of the Lord
standing at the threshing floor on Mount Moriah? Did he know
that this was the very mount on which Abraham, in obedience to
God, had offered up Isaac? Was David's heart smitten by
Abraham's obedience and God's response of covenantal love?
Whatever the case, David buys the threshing floor of Araunah,
builds an altar, and sacrifices a burnt offering to the Lord.

David said to him [Araunah], *"Let me have the site of
your threshing floor so I can build an altar to the Lord,*

that the plague on the people may be stopped. Sell it to me at the full price." Araunah said to David, "Take it! Let my lord the king do whatever pleases him. Look, I will give the oxen...the threshing sledges...and the wheat....I will give all this." But King David replied to Araunah, "No, I insist on paying the full price. I will not take for the Lord what is yours, or sacrifice a burnt offering that costs me nothing." So David paid Araunah...[and] *built an altar to the Lord there....He called on the Lord, and the Lord answered him with fire from heaven on the altar of burnt offering. Then the Lord spoke to the angel, and he put his sword back into its sheath* (1 Chronicles 21:22-27).

No wonder David refused to take the field without paying for it. God was stopping at Mount Moriah, the site of great sacrifice! Perhaps this was a window of mercy. Perhaps this mountain would again be a place of God's merciful blessing if he, David, would bring a sacrificial offering to God.

So David builds an altar on the ground of historic visitation, paying the full price for both the land and the animals for the burnt offerings. Then he calls "on the Lord, and the Lord answered him with fire from heaven on the altar of burnt offering" (1 Chron. 21:26b).

God answers with fire from Heaven, and a new generation receives the Father's inheritance of a visitation of mercy. By paying the full price, David secured the full blessing, a blessing that would reach beyond the years of his life into the life of King Solomon, his son.

Years later the temple of Solomon was built on the very place where David had sacrificed burnt offerings to the Lord.[4] As King Solomon stood before the altar of the Lord in the completed temple, he prayed,

..."O Lord, God of Israel, there is no God like You in heaven or on earth—You who keep Your covenant of love with Your servants who continue wholeheartedly in Your way. You have kept Your promise to Your servant David my

*father.... And now, O Lord, God of Israel, let Your word
that You promised Your servant David come true. ...give
attention to Your servant's prayer and his plea for mercy,
O Lord my God.... May Your eyes be open toward this
temple day and night.... Hear the supplications of Your
servant and of Your people Israel when they pray toward
this place. Hear from heaven, Your dwelling place; and
when You hear, forgive"* (2 Chronicles 6:14-21).

Do you see what Solomon prays? He appeals to the
covenant of his forefathers, calls on God to dwell in a special
way in the specific location where Abraham offered up Isaac
and where David paid the full price, and asks that forgiveness
be released whenever God hears the prayers of His people.
When Solomon finished praying, fire came down from Heaven
and consumed the burnt offerings, and the glory of the Lord
filled the temple.

Glory and fire—these are the covenantal blessings of a
covenantal God; and they were sent to the very place that had
previously seen divine fire fall in response to the sacrificial
giving of man. My contention is this: God's heart is moved by
sacrifice. He always sends fire—revival fire, if you will—on
acceptable sacrifices. So every place where revival has been in
the past can experience revival today if the new generation will
do as their forefathers have done, offering themselves on the
altar of worship and consecration.

History reveals the truth of this reality: Angeles Temple,
where divine fire fell in the 1920's, is only blocks from Bonnie
Brae Street, the birthplace of the Azusa Street Revival in 1906;
Mott Auditorium, the home of Harvest Rock Church and the
site of the great Nazarene revival in years past, was again visited by the fire of God in 1995 and continues to be a place
where the presence and power of God are being poured out.
The question is, will our generation again see more places
where God's covenantal fire is poured out because His true
sons and daughters renew the covenant by sacrifices of love?

Rick Joyner, in his prophetic word entitled "The Bridge to Revival," saw a place named "The Dream Center" that would be used for revival in Los Angeles. Interestingly, The Dream Center is an inner city ministry birthed by Tommy Barnett and his son Matthew that is just beginning to explode with the blessing of God. It is located only a few blocks away from both Angeles Temple (where Aimee Semple McPherson ushered in a historic move of God and the Foursquare Church) and the site of the Azusa Street Revival.

There is a historic altar, a historic well, in downtown Los Angeles. Similar altars and wells exist across our land. But "America is spiritually dying because God has sales reps and not channels of His glory. We feverishly do the right things, almost as a bribe to postpone the needed pouring out of ourselves on God as a living sacrifice."[5]

I'm tired of doing good stuff. I pray that you are too. It's time to renew the covenants and offer sacrifices that please God. May those of you who know your spiritual inheritance kindle your faith so that these altars may again receive the divine fire of God and these wells may again supply the refreshing flow of God's presence we so desperately need. Make every effort to discover the forgotten people and places God has visited in years past. We will see God's presence and power in these places of our inheritance; as He remembers the past sacrifices of love, His great heart will erupt, and His mercy will spill over.

May we be the generation who appeals to the covenants of our forefathers, who call on God to revisit the places He has visited in the past, and who lay extravagant sacrifices of love on altars of trust and obedience. Then perchance God's heart will be moved, He will remember His covenant, and He will send fire and glory, the full blessings of His covenant. May we be people who not only take the Lord's covenant on our lips but also live it.

Chapter 5

God Is Seeking Covenant Friends

The Power of Covenant

In 1977, while going to seminary in Ashland, Ohio, I met a young man named Duke Smith. Duke had just become a Christian and was on fire for the Lord. I was much older than he, but we were joined together in spirit. We made a covenant together that we would seek the outpouring of Acts chapter 2 until we found it.

That covenant supernaturally led us to Maryland, where the Holy Spirit was moving on a people called "Gathering of Believers," led by Larry Tomczak and C.J. Mahaney. Because of the covenant, I left everything, even my future as a pastor in my denomination, which my grandfather six generations before had founded. I exchanged the opportunity to become a pastor in the Brethren in Christ Church for five years of mopping hospital floors, mowing lawns, and sweeping boiler rooms. But those years were wonderful. The broom closet became my prayer closet. I would worship God in my little closet as I rinsed out my mop. I would sing and pray in tongues behind the 52-inch lawn mower, weeping because of

God's love for me. I would hear God's inner voice tell me in the boiler room, "I've called you as an instrument of revival!"

My friend Duke Smith moved away and I lost touch with him for 12 years. Then, when I moved to Pasadena to plant a church, I unexpectedly received a phone call. It was Duke—I couldn't believe it. He was living in Rosemead, the town right next to Pasadena. He had gone through 12 dark years away from the Lord.

But God remembered our covenant promises. He had bound us together with cords that could not be broken. So He led us individually through 12 years and 3000 miles to bring us to the same place at the beginning of the renewal in 1994. About that time, Duke began to seek God. Later he told me, "Lou, when I became a Christian, I had prophetic dreams all the time. But I haven't had any for 12 years. Last night I had a dream in which I was flying in the air, leading worship in a huge building with huge double doors in the back."

When the renewal moved to Mott Auditorium, Duke was astonished. Mott was the building in his dream! Today Duke is one of our worship leaders at Harvest Rock Church and we are pursuing the covenant that we made nearly 20 years ago.

Covenant making. When I met Duke in 1977, I knew very little of the depth of commitment involved in such a relationship. Through the life parable of my friendship with Duke, God has taught me much about His covenant faithfulness. He will not fail. His promises are altogether dependable. Despite our faithlessness, He is totally faithful. He has locked onto us in love. Even if He must take us 3000 miles and through 12 years of darkness, He remembers heartfelt covenant and works on our behalf to fulfill those promises.

Jonathan and David knew this devotion. David loved Jonathan as himself.[1] The two were bound together not only for their lifetimes but beyond the temporal into the eternal. Generations were blessed because of their covenant. Years after Jonathan had been killed in battle, King David remembers his friend. His heart is deeply moved because of the great love they had shared. Suddenly the covenant he had made with Jonathan comes to his mind. He remembers his oath, "The Lord is witness between you and me, and between your descendants and my descendants forever" (1 Sam. 20:42b); so "David ask[s], 'Is there anyone still left of the house of Saul to whom I can show kindness for Jonathan's sake?' " (2 Sam. 9:1) When he is told that only one of Jonathan's sons remains, a crippled man named Mephibosheth, who in the natural is totally unqualified to sit at the king's table, David, from the passion of his love for Jonathan, shows kindness to Jonathan's son.

> *When Mephibosheth son of Jonathan, the son of Saul, came to David, he bowed down to pay him honor.... "Don't be afraid," David said to him, "for I will surely show you kindness for the sake of your father Jonathan. I will restore to you all the land that belonged to your grandfather Saul, and you will always eat at my table"* (2 Samuel 9:6-7).

As I read these words, tears come to my eyes. Maybe this is what God is saying in Heaven today. Maybe as He remembers Jonathan Edwards, the father of the first great awakening in America, He asks, "Is there anyone still left in his family, in his nation, that I can show mercy to for Jonathan Edwards' sake?" Though we are crippled with sin and have lost the inheritance of our cities to the devil, God may yet show mercy and restore us. This is the hope of America—God keeping His covenant with our godly ancestors.

Because God is a covenant God, those with whom He makes a covenant become His special friends, and He makes a distinction between these special friends and other people. He backs up these covenantal friends like no others. Who are these people with whom He has eternally bonded? They are the men and women of all ages who have walked with Him, choosing obedience over popularity. They are every upper-room gathering throughout history that has opened the heavens through prayer. They are every "holy club," such as those started on college campuses by John Wesley and George Whitefield. They are every lone lover and worshiper, pouring out his or her fragrance on Heaven!

The Nature of Covenant

Unfortunately, Americans know little of the nature of covenant. Unlike most Eastern nations, who are familiar with covenant making, the practice of making and keeping covenant has been lost somewhere in the archives of our history. Look at all the treaties with the American Indians that we have broken. As one anointed teacher said, "America is a most uncivilized country because it knows nothing of the blood covenant. Our pattern of breaking treaties was incomprehensible to the Indians. They simply could not understand how anyone could break a covenant."

The word *covenant* means "to bond or fit together." The ritual of covenant making often included the following elements.

1. The participants would cut an animal in two and walk between the two bloody parts. By doing this they were declaring that the two were becoming one spirit and were demonstrating what would happen to the party who broke the covenant, that is he would be cut in two, as was the animal. Abraham cut a heifer, a goat, and a ram into two pieces each and arranged the halves opposite each other. After dusk "a smoking firepot with a blazing torch appeared and passed between the pieces" (Gen. 15:17b).

2. The two parties would read the promises and blessings of keeping the covenant, as well as the curses that would be called down upon the party who broke the covenant.

3. The participants would make vows to each other.

4. The participants would exchange garments, gifts, rings, swords, or other items of value. This was a symbolic

way of saying, "What is mine is yours, and what is yours is mine. If someone attacks you, they become my enemy and my sword will defend you."

5. A physical mark (in Abraham's case, circumcision[2]) is made on the body of each participant as a sign that they have become "covenant brothers." The ceremony was not complete and the designation "friend" was not used until this marking had been performed.

6. Feasting followed the covenant ceremony.

7. From the time of the covenant, neither party would speak evil of the other.

8. Covenants usually lasted beyond the lifetime of the participants to future generations. God promises that the covenant will be not only with Abraham, but with his descendants forever.[3]

These components of a covenant relationship are evident throughout the friendship between God and Abraham. God says to Abraham, "Give Me your son," and Abraham is bound by covenant to do so. As a blood brother of God, he must obey. But then God is bound by the very nature of the same covenant to fulfil His promises as well—including the provision of His own Son to meet our great need for atonement. Abraham receives in his body the sign of the covenant, but where is God's scar to prove it? The bloody wounds of Jesus are the covenantal marks that guarantee God is indeed a covenant partner, and as such, will keep His covenant promises.

The Promise of Covenant

The thought that God would enter into such a binding agreement with a man is staggering. That He would be willing to forever seal His part of it by His own horrible death, is nearly incomprehensible. Surely the covenant confirmed by so great a sacrifice must be accompanied by magnificent promises. And it is! In Genesis, God promises Abraham land, descendants, and protection. But when Paul comments on this transaction in the

New Testament, he doesn't even mention these things as the blessings that Abraham received. Instead he writes, "He redeemed us in order that the blessing given to Abraham might come to the Gentiles through Christ Jesus, so that by faith we might receive the promise of the Spirit" (Gal. 3:14). Time and again in the New Testament, the promise that we receive through the covenant with Abraham, sealed by the death and resurrection of Jesus, is the Holy Spirit! And through Christ, even Gentiles may receive Him.

I am reminded here of a young friend, Abbott, who learned quite powerfully in early 1998 that the power of the Holy Spirit is released through the covenant in Jesus' blood. He and his wife were seeking God with great hunger for their own spiritual wells to be opened. Although they had experienced charismatic encounters, they wanted the baptism of the Spirit with the kind of power that is described in the Bible.

One evening, as they prayerfully studied some passages of Scripture pertaining to covenant, Abbott came upon Zechariah 9:11: "As for you, because of the blood of My covenant with you, I will free your prisoners from the waterless pit." Jesus' definition of water is the Holy Spirit: " 'Whoever believes in Me, as the Scripture has said, streams of living water will flow from within him.' By this He meant the Spirit, whom those who believed in Him were later to receive" (Jn. 7:38-39a).

Suddenly a simple revelation exploded within my friend's heart. He saw that it was the blood of the New Covenant that would free him from his own waterless pit and open up the baptism of the Holy Spirit, the streams of living water of which Jesus had spoken. Boldness overtook my friend to claim this promise of the Spirit on the basis of Jesus' shed blood. Kneeling down to pray, he was instantaneously baptized with power, as shock waves of electricity knocked him to the ground and he began to speak in other tongues. In fact, for two hours he could not speak English! He broke forth in what neighbors, who overheard his loud praises, said were Russian and Polish. The covenant of Jesus' blood had opened the door to Acts 1:8: "But you will receive power when the Holy Spirit comes on you; and you will be My witnesses in Jerusalem, and in all Judea and Samaria, and to the ends of the earth."

The next day my friend witnessed to an old man who espoused Darwinism and had resisted the gospel for years. This hardened opponent of Jesus Christ broke immediately at the witness of my friend and surrendered to Christ.

One person with his or her own well open can release water to a whole community. Jesus said to the Samaritan woman at the well, "...whoever drinks the water I give him will never thirst. Indeed, the water I give him will become in him a spring of water welling up to eternal life" (Jn. 4:14). When this woman opened her heart and experienced a gush of the water in her life, her whole town was affected and they, too, got to taste it. "Many of the Samaritans from that town believed in Him because of the woman's testimony..." (Jn. 4:39). If we would see revival in our land, we must return to the blood covenant of the Lord Jesus Christ. It is this covenant that releases the springs of living water that can water an entire community when it gushes forth.

The blood of Jesus is the guarantee of an outpouring of the Spirit, both individually and corporately: "Having believed, you were marked in Him with a seal, the promised Holy Spirit" (Eph. 1:13b). If revival is nothing less than the pervasive work of the wonderful Holy Spirit, surely we can tug on these covenantal promises with great faith and boldness to see Him come! I want to stir your hearts to outrageous faith! Do you believe the words of Jesus: "I am going to send you what My Father has promised; but stay in the city until you have been clothed with power from on high" (Lk. 24:49)? Do you believe that a glorious second Pentecost will again sweep the earth? Or do your prayers reflect a meager expectation?

The Jews: The People of Covenant

God is searching for people who will covenant with Him through the blood of the Lord Jesus Christ and through their commitment to reopen the wells of their spiritual heritage.

These spiritual wells begin with the Jews, the people with whom God first established covenant. As the Scripture says concerning the Jews: "As far as the gospel is concerned, they are enemies on your account; but as far as election is concerned, they are loved on account of the patriarchs, for God's gifts and His call are irrevocable" (Rom. 11:28-29). The covenant promises to Abraham, Isaac, and Jacob are irrevocable. They will be fulfilled.

So let us first dig the wells of revival by returning to our Jewish roots, to know and follow the ways and obedience of Abraham, Isaac, and Jacob.

> *Look to the rock from which you were cut and to the quarry from which you were hewn; look to Abraham, your father, and to Sarah, who gave you birth. When I called him he was but one, and I blessed him and made him many. The Lord will surely comfort Zion and will look with compassion on all her ruins; He will make her deserts like Eden, her wastelands like the garden of the Lord. Joy and gladness will be found in her, thanksgiving and the sound of singing* (Isaiah 51:1b-3).

Here, Isaiah is calling the remnant to return to their roots, to know and follow their spiritual fathers' ways of worship, sacrifice, faith, and obedience.

Let us pray for Israel with great faith, calling on the promises of the Holy Spirit on their behalf. Since the promises hold true for us as Gentiles, how much more for them! Now is the time to see a harvest among God's chosen people. The day when "all Israel will be saved" (Rom. 11:26) is rapidly approaching. May more Jews be saved in this century than in all others combined since the first century. This is their destiny! When we begin to redig the wells of our inheritance, may we never forget that the first wells were dug by Abraham and that we are participants in the covenant because of God's great mercy toward us: "For I tell you that Christ has become a servant of the Jews on behalf of God's truth, to confirm the promises made to the patriarchs so that the Gentiles may glorify God for His mercy..." (Rom. 15:8-9).

Evoking the Memory of the Covenant

Covenantal relationships are serious commitments. They must be born in the heart by God before they are initiated in the natural. My friendship with Chris Berglund is one such relationship. God sent Chris to me in 1984, months after I moved to Pasadena to plant a church there. We would pray together for revival at 4:30 in the morning. Many sleepless nights found our hearts burning together seeking God. Over the years, I've found my heart moved to tears for the great joy of having a friend like Chris. What affection we experience—even the affections of Christ. In almost every big moment of my life since 1984, whether in a time of discouragement or a time of decision-making, Chris has called me with the exact word or revelation that I have needed. He's been a prophet to me. Like Jonathan and David, our hearts are joined together and we are one in spirit.[4] How has such a journey occurred? Through a mutual covenant! Chris and I covenanted together early in our relationship to "seek the Lord, the God of [our] fathers, with all [our] heart and soul" (2 Chron. 15:12b). In many ways this book is the fruit of that covenant.

Some covenant partners are contemporaries, such as Chris and I, and Frank Bartleman and his prayer partner, William Boehmer, who covenanted together in 1905 to become covenant warriors for revival. Other covenant partnerships reach through the years to unite the hearts of men and of women who never physically meet. In some measure, God knit me with Frank Bartleman's covenanted inheritance.

One day I stood in the Pasadena Public Library trying to hide my sobbing in that quiet place. I had just been reading about Frank Bartleman's life, and suddenly it was as if the lights went on. Why did my heart burn so hot when I read about this holy man? Why were these longings so deeply stirred within me as I read the revival history of Pasadena and

Los Angeles? In many ways I had entered into his covenants. Our hearts burned for the same thing. We both wanted to see Pasadena given wholly to God.

John Dawson, a man who has deeply moved my heart, had an experience similar to that which I had with Bartleman. He said,

> "One of the most moving experiences in my life was standing in the room where David Livingstone was born....As I looked through the relics of his life and read of his struggle for Africa, I thought, Surely God will bless Scotland because of this man. Even as I write these words, I am overtaken with weeping because my own ancestors came from this land. Oh, what a heritage undergirds my life as a missionary."[5]

If such emotion fills our hearts as we think of the devotion to the Lord of men like Bartleman and Livingstone, how great must be God's affection when He remembers these covenantal friends and their sacrifice. The key to this intense response dropped into my heart while I was talking one day with John Dawson. "Lou," John said, "covenant is much more than a sterile, legal transaction. God's covenants are covenants of divine passion initiated with those who have moved His great heart. Therefore when we pray, 'Lord, remember David,' it evokes such memories in the Father of the man after His own heart, that He cannot contain Himself. These memories stir Him to act."

God's Diary of Love

The book *Azusa Street* by Frank Bartleman is not merely a collection of one man's thoughts and actions recorded for posterity on how they reached revival. It is God's book of memories, His diary of love. The annals of history are filled with the accounts of sacrifices and of saints who so moved God's heart that He recorded them in His diary of love, saying, "Bring Me My diary, My book of memories. Write down their names so that they may live forever before Me! These are the ones who have captured My heart. These are Mine, My treasured possession. In the Day of Judgment, I'll set them apart from all the world. I'll spare them, these who are My friends. Upon these I will pour My Holy Spirit."

Malachi, under the prophetic spirit, witnessed God's response to a band of radical worshipers. His was a covenant-breaking generation. Complaints against God were widespread. Yet this fellowship of God's people gathered together to seek mutual encouragement.

> *Then those who feared the Lord talked with each other, and the Lord listened and heard. A scroll of remembrance was written in His presence concerning those who feared the Lord and honored His name. "They will be mine," says the Lord Almighty, "in the day when I make up My treasured possession. I will spare them, just as in compassion a man spares his son who serves him. And you will again see the distinction between the righteous and the wicked, between those who serve God and those who do not"* (Malachi 3:16-18).

God's scroll of remembrance is not simply a reminder of things past, for He is not a God who forgets and needs a book to recall people, places, and events. No, God's book of memories is His diary of love, recording the names and deeds of those who have stirred His heart. He remembers what lays hold of His heart. And just what evokes remembrance responses from the heart of God? In a word, devotion.

Strategies alone will never bring revival because revival is the eruption of God's heart on a life poured out. It's the Father's response to those who have been His lovers and to whom He gave promises and sent fire on their offerings. These faithful ones passed into glory and eternal reward. Then there arose another generation, a generation of great-grandsons and great-granddaughters "...who knew neither the Lord nor what He had done for Israel [His people]" (Judg. 2:10). One day one of these granddaughters finds a book among the old heirlooms and the prized possessions of her grandmother stored in the attic. The book is her grandmother's diary, the stories of a woman of great devotion who prayed three hours a day for her little country church until the Holy Spirit came and shook that church and the surrounding township. As the young girl reads, she begins to burn inside, saying, "This is my heritage. Wow! This isn't happening in my church. Maybe it could!" Then as the tears fall from her eyes and stain the pages of the old diary, the young girl begins to pour herself out on God, and another memorial is made.

Jesus spoke of such love relationships of costly devotion. When a woman poured a jar of expensive perfume on His head while He was eating, the disciples complained about the waste; but Jesus rebuked them, saying,

> *Why are you bothering this woman? She has done a beautiful thing to Me. The poor you will always have with you, but you will not always have Me. When she poured this perfume on My body, she did it to prepare Me for burial. I tell you the truth, wherever this gospel is preached throughout the world, what she has done will also be told, in memory of her* (Matthew 26:10b-13).

For all time and eternity, the Lord Jesus made a memorial to one who loved Him so profoundly. In effect, He shouted, "This is what moves My heart: devotion." Devotion is what covenant making with God is all about: "I remember the devotion of your youth, how as a bride you loved Me…" (Jer. 2:2). Notice, God doesn't say that He remembers our hard work for Him, our ministries, or our mega churches with great programs. What He remembers is our devotion to Him, the longing of our hearts for Him, our total abandonment to live before Him in holiness and to commune in secret with Him. This is what pulls on God's heartstrings.

Likewise, the greatest sadness in the Father's heart comes when we stop loving Him.

*I know your deeds, your hard work and your perseverance.
… You have persevered and have endured hardships for My
name, and have not grown weary. Yet I hold this against
you: You have forsaken your first love. Remember*
[because this is what God remembers] *the height from
which you have fallen! Repent and do the things you did
at first. If you do not repent, I will come to you and remove
your lampstand from its place* (Revelation 2:2-5).

It is not a lack of *works* but a lack of *longing* in their hearts
for Him that Jesus addresses when He commands John to
write concerning the church of Ephesus. He remembers the
first days of Ephesus and the love that was there. What a holy
visitation they received in those days! Then they succumbed to
the treadmill of religious activity, forsaking God for their
"busyness." The pain God feels when His people lose their
first love for Him is also revealed in the words of the prophet
Jeremiah:

*"Be appalled at this, O heavens, and shudder with great
horror," declares the Lord. "My people have committed
two sins: They have forsaken Me, the spring of living
water, and have dug their own cisterns, broken cisterns
that cannot hold water"* (Jeremiah 2:12-13).

Jesus' command to His disciples during His last supper
with them comes also to us. "Do this in remembrance of Me"
(Lk. 22:19b). The word *remembrance* (Greek, *anamnesis*) is a
passionate appeal for the disciples to keep the depth of Jesus'
covenantal love for them and His commitment to them ever
engraved in the center of their affections.

Covenant Will Open the Door

Appealing to the covenant is more powerful than prayer. In
prayer, one may plead effectively with God for answers, but in
covenant the partner becomes the very altar on which the fire
falls. We must not lose sight of the fact that Jesus' death on the
cross was the true covenantal act. "During the days of [His]
life on earth, He offered up prayers and petitions with loud

cries and tears to the one who could save Him from death, and He was heard because of His reverent submission" (Heb. 5:7). His prayers were effective only in as much as they sprang from a body laid down as a living sacrifice.

There is glory that is yet to be revealed through mutual covenants between men and women, and between God and His people. Chris Berglund received a dream that confirms this truth. Chris said, "In the dream, I saw the brilliant glory of God behind a cracked door. Then I turned to you, Lou, and asked, 'What will open the door to God's glory?' Then, as I saw a little combination lock and a hand that dialed a combination, I heard a voice say, 'Covenant will open the door.' "

Others in the Body of Christ are hearing the same thing. As Francis Frangipane says, "In talking with national and international prayer leaders, I find many are hearing a similar word: the Lord is calling His people to unite with Him in covenant power for the nation! Of course we will never supersede Christ's covenant. However, by picking up our cross, we are called to extend the redemptive power of Christ's cross into our world and times."[6]

The covenants that I must renew will be different from those you must renew because our heritage and experience are different. Whereas God has given me a measure of faith to covenant with Him for Los Angeles, as did Frank Bartleman in the beginning of the twentieth century, I do not have the same covenantal faith for New York City. That may be your covenant to renew. Make a covenant with God within the sphere where He has extended your faith, then discover the history of revival in that area. Find the stories of men and women of faith who have covenanted with God in years gone by for that area and tug on God's heartstrings by reminding Him of these lovers of God who have devoted themselves to Him on the altar of love.

This pulling on the cords of God's heart through remembrance prayer appears to be an important gift God has given us to bring revival to our land. Just as a mother cannot forget the baby at her breast, so God cannot forget those whom He has loved and to whom He has bound Himself. His memories of them are engraved on the palms of His hands, and every time He looks at His hand, He remembers with deep feeling their love and sacrificial devotion.[7]

Let us learn to evoke the memory of the covenant, praying as a descendant of King David prayed in Psalm 132, appealing for God's blessings on a new generation because of God's memories of David and His covenant of love with him: "O God, remember David, remember all his troubles! ... 'Honor your servant David; don't disdain your anointed one.' God gave David His word, He won't back out on this promise" (Ps. 132:1,10-11a TM).

May we be these covenantal friends whose names are written in God's book of memories, being etched on the very palms of His hands. May our covenantal love and devotion be like that of King David—for God, and for those whom He sends into our lives as covenant friends.

Chapter 6

An Open Heaven

Walking the Highway of the King

In March 1995, a band of 30 intercessors started a journey from San Diego to just north of San Francisco, some 500 miles away, walking an average of 15 miles a day. I was part of this group. Our route followed El Camino Real (The Highway of the King). El Camino Real is the original missions highway from San Diego to San Francisco, blazed to link the missions stations that became the foundation cities of California. The route we walked included winding streets whose names still hint at their historic roots, as well as parts of U.S. Route 101.

I first heard of this pilgrimage when I received a visit from my dear friend, Steve Hawthorne. Steve invited me to join a band of intercessors in "prayer-walking"[1] the entire length of El Camino Real. Our task was to pray along this historic route in 40 days (March 1 through April 9, 1995). We walked as we prayed in repentance for the sins committed throughout California's history. We were even more fixed on California's destiny, so we prayed in hope of reclaiming God's missionary

purpose embedded in the beginnings of the state, and to prepare the way of the Lord for a great visitation to our cities.

California's early history became very real to me as Steve
talked. The founding heritage of California is in these 21 missions along El Camino Real. The founding father who established them was Father Junípero Serra, a man with remarkable
missionary zeal. Junípero Serra embodied a passion for missions that was alive in many Spaniards of his day. These
Catholic missionaries carried a distinctive, genuine love for
God and a heartfelt apostolic passion that every nation be
impacted for Christ.

> "When José de Galvez [the governmental representative
> of Spain to Mexico from 1765–1771], told Serra of his
> determination to occupy Alta California [now known as
> Southern California], the Mallorcan friar immediately
> offered to go in person as the first volunteer 'to erect the
> holy standard of the cross in Monterey.' He assured
> Galvez that other missionaries would not be lacking to
> join in that great enterprise. This was the opportunity
> Serra had longed and prayed for—to reach pagan land and
> plant there the Faith on unworked soil. It was, after all, the
> reason Serra had come to America."[2]

In his first letter from Alta California, Fray Junípero Serra
had a timely piece of advice and warning: "Let those who are
to come here as missionaries not imagine that they are coming
for any other purpose but to endure hardships for the love of
God and for the salvation of souls."[3] In a letter written to offi-
cials at the Apostolic College of San Fernando, Serra repeated
his qualifications for future priestly volunteers in the area:
"Those who come here dedicated to so holy a work must
undergo sacrifices, as everyone knows… In these distant parts,
one must expect to suffer some hardship, but these will be even
more burdensome to those who are seeking every convenience
and comfort." What Fray Junípero Serra looked for in others
was, in himself, taken for granted.[4]

These early missionaries journeyed, suffered, and planted in the land they came to love, working among the native peoples whom they had come to die for. In 1773, on his second missionary journey, "Serra asked his brethren to commend him to God for they would never see his face again. His biographer later wrote, 'He touched the hearts of all in such a way that they shed copious tears. They were edified at his great humility and fervor in undertaking so long a journey at an advanced age and in such poor health that he was almost unable to stand.' He was off again, but not before writing to his nephew to report that, 'I am restored to health and brought back...and feel ready to set out on my journey back to that vineyard of the Lord.' "5

On November 4, 1775, a group of Indians attacked and killed Father Luis Jayme at the mission in San Diego. The reaction of Father Serra to the news of his comrade's death speaks volumes about the attitudes of the early friars. Far from being disappointed and saddened, Father Serra said, "Thanks be to God; now that the terrain has been watered by blood, the conversion of the San Diego Indians will take place."6 His words echo the famous words of Tertullian, an early Church father, who said, "The blood of the martyrs is the seed of the Church."7 Immediately after this massacre, Serra wrote to the Viceroy asking for mercy for the Indians, reminding the Viceroy "that in case the Indians, whether pagans or Christians would kill me, they should be pardoned."8

Unfortunately not all Spaniards who came to the New World shared Father Serra's apostolic view of sacrifice, and not all Spanish influence on California's soil was godly. Often the missions became outposts of Spanish imperialism from which the native people were oppressed. The common misconception of the colonial era was that before one could "Christianize" pagans, one had to first "civilize" them. This well-intentioned zeal to produce what was thought to be a superior and godly culture resulted in a total, and often severe, subjugation of the Indians. Some Indians genuinely turned to Christ, but many more conversions were the result of coercion. In fact, many native Californians suffered a virtual state of slavery as the padres enforced a Spanish lifestyle with a strict regime. The native peoples also suffered greatly, and their population plummeted drastically during the time of the missions and the years immediately following, because of the introduction of European diseases and the interruption of conventional native lifestyles.

Nevertheless, the fact remains that California was founded in Christian missions. This heritage has continued in recent generations, with missions activity from this state being far greater than from most other places in America. Many worldwide ministries have been birthed here. My interest was therefore aroused by my friend's vision. (El Camino Real is such an awesome covenantal name! Father Serra's description of California as the "vineyard of the Lord" is likewise a covenantal name, prophesying of the fruitfulness that would spring from this state.)

Steve and a friend, Mike Griffiths, had much earlier taken two weeks to traverse the entire walking route by car. They were mapping the exact route and checking the logistics of doing the entire route from San Diego to San Francisco in 40 days. Near the end of the journey, both of them became extremely discouraged. Was this what God wanted them to do? Was it even physically possible to do it in 40 days? They were on the verge of canceling the entire effort. At the moment of deepest discouragement, they went on as they had planned, to visit the Carmel Mission near Monterey early on Sunday morning before services began. But when they arrived, church services had already begun. At the very moment they both sofly stepped in the doors of the old, hallowed halls, the priest slowly and boldly read the Scripture in the liturgy for the morning: "And the angel of the Lord came back the second time, and touched him, and said, 'Arise and eat, because the journey is too great for you.' " Steve and Mike were stunned. They were utterly daunted by a journey that appeared to be too great for them. The priest read more: "So he arose, and ate and drank; and he went in the strength of that food forty days and forty nights as far as Horeb, the mountain of God" (1 Kings 19:7-8 NKJV). They both stumbled out the door into the courtyard, needing to hear no more. God couldn't have spoken more powerfully. What were the odds of hearing the only Scripture reference to a journey of 40 days at the point that they were most discouraged? And that it should be a word about Elijah announced at Carmel Mission, named for the very mountain Elijah had just come from in the story. The Lord was sealing His call that He wanted to reclaim the original apostolic mantle of Californa, since it is also at Carmel Mission that Father Serra lies buried. Steve and Mike were committed to follow through. I was truly honored to join them in this quest and to walk with them for 17 of the 40 days.

As we walked the El Camino Real, we worshiped, interceded, and proclaimed that the road's true purpose was to be the Highway of the King of kings, not of a long-dead Spanish king. It was for the Lord that the road had been named. Each day we prayed prayers of repentance, identifying in a biblical sense with those who had lived before us and asking for forgiveness for the sins that had been committed in the geographical locations we walked through. Forty days later, April 9, 1995 (Palm Sunday), the prayer team arrived in San Francisco, prophetically declaring the welcoming of renewal to our cities. "Blessed is He who comes in the name of the Lord..." (Mt. 21:9b).[9]

Prophesying to Demonic Strongholds

Of the great distance we covered and the significant places through which we passed on the journey, one place really captured my attention. Built right beside the original path of the El Camino Real, a Rosicrucian New Age healing temple stood, facing east. This place is where healing "elder spirits" are said to reside. No person is allowed to enter the building. The walls and surrounding walkways are covered with occultic, astrological, and Masonic symbols. There is also a sanitarium where people come to live while they are waiting for the spirits to heal them. A large pentagram, laid out with a cross in the center, provides a focal point of spiritual invitation to demons.

At the turn of the century, the founder of this New Age temple had received specific instructions from "a being of light" to come to America, to search out the exact location this "being" had described, and to establish this center on that location. A burning passion gripped my heart as I stood on this ground dedicated to satan. From its strategical position on a hill in Oceanside, the elevation of which permits it to dominate the whole valley, it casts a dark shadow over the area. As I stood within this sphere of darkness, I prophesied in prayer what I believed to be God's heart for this place: Some day, that center now devoted to evil would become a 24-hour house of worship and prayer; it would become a place devoted to God to release the true gift of healing from the Holy Spirit and to restore the entire valley; and the once holy mission road established and traveled by the early apostles of California would not be blocked or hindered by these demonic principalities and powers.

The Keys of David

Three years later, the Lord initiated, in somewhat of a strange way, a fresh commissioning of authority for me to pray again for California and to reclaim that particular hill. Wherever I turned, it seemed that I saw the numbers 222. At first I thought nothing of it, but the reoccurence of these numbers became so outrageous and so obvious that I began to inquire if the Lord was trying to get my attention.

In January of 1998, I was invited to hold meetings in Oceanside. Because of the generosity of our hosts, I planned to take my whole family to a beach hotel. As we got into the car and I turned the key, the time on the van clock was 2:22. I said to my family, "There's that number again!" The kids laughed, but I pondered it in my heart. At the hotel, the desk clerk handed me the key to my hotel room…room 222.

Suddenly the spirit of prophecy began stirring in me and Isaiah 22:22 burst into my spirit, "I will place on his shoulder the key to the house of David; what he opens no one can shut, and what he shuts no one can open." Deep in my spirit, a fresh sincere faith began to stir in me for California. The memory of the prayer walk flooded into my mind, and I felt the Spirit say that it was time for the heavens over California to open, and that I would be given a key to help open it. I also sensed that Oceanside and the Rosicrucian center would be strategic in this.

In mid January, John and Paula Sanford held a conference at Harvest Rock Church. During a time of deep prayer and repentance with our leadership team and the Sanfords, the Holy Spirit spoke so clearly to me, "Lou, it's also Genesis 22:2, '…"Take your son, your only son Isaac, whom you love, and go to the region of Moriah. Sacrifice him there as a burnt offering on one of the mountains I will tell you about." ' " Instantly I knew what the Lord was saying: "Lay down Rock the Nations."

Rock the Nations is a wonderful youth ministry led by Gary Black in Colorado Springs. It is dedicated to releasing the Father heart of God and raising up prayer revival and missions among American youth. God had allowed me to be part of birthing the ministry with Rusty Carlson when it was released in a more public sense in Pasadena in 1994. Now He was saying to me, "Lay down your Isaac, the ministry you love. Stop traveling all over the country for Rock the Nations. Confine your traveling to southern California, between Sacramento and San Diego. Come home and fight for Los Angeles and for California."

Laying down my involvement with Rock the Nations was a difficult, painful decision. I wrestled with it. One day as I was listening to a tape in my car on the blood covenant, Kenneth Copeland was speaking on Abraham's sacrifice of

Isaac. I could hardly take it as the Spirit witnessed again to my heart concerning the choice I had to make. Unable to listen anymore, I pulled out the tape. The car clock instantly came on...2:22. Two days later, I laid down my part in the ministry of Rock the Nations, but committed to be a father to them in intercession.

The following weekend in Sacramento, just before I stood up to preach, a sister's prophetic word jolted me again. She said, "Lou, it's Second Samuel, chapter 22" (David's covenantal victories over his enemies). Again the number 222! That weekend I experienced more authority than I'd ever known in preaching concerning the future of California. Obedience releases authority. You gain covenantal favor with God. I'd given Him my Isaac; now He was giving me the promise!

A few weeks later, revival evangelist Tommy Tenney, I, and some 50 intercessors went to Bonnie Brae Street, where the Azusa Street Revival had started. There we drove a stake into the ground, declaring that this revival well in Los Angeles would again burst forth. Moments after this powerful time of reclaiming our inheritance, I got into my car and turned the key. The clock again came on to 2:22. "What You open, no one can shut! Oh God, open the wells!" I cried.

Tearing Down the High Places

Later that spring, in April 1998, the Lord led me to take a team of 27 intercessors from Harvest International Ministries churches across southern California to meet with the Oceanside intercessors, led by Pastor Mike Hubbard, for a time of seeking God. We wanted to turn the prayer keys for an opening of the heavens over that valley and the shutting of the gates of hell over the Rosicrucian center. Ironically, a wonderful Spirit-filled monastery faces the Rosicrucian center on the opposite side of the valley. While the majority of the intercessors stayed in the monastery to cover us in prayer and to shout "Grace, grace" to the Rosicrucian center on the other side, seven of us went to this den of evil to exercise the authority of Heaven over the gates of hell.

Earlier that morning, the Lord had given us the Scripture of Zechariah 4:7 that says, "What are you, O mighty mountain? Before Zerubbabel you will become level ground. Then he will bring out the capstone to shouts of 'God bless it! God bless it!' " [Or "Grace, grace to it!" as the New American Standard Bible translates it.] Our task was to look beyond what this hill had become and to call forth the divine destiny that the Lord has purposed for this place—a destiny, I believe, that includes the establishment of a major prayer and worship center. That day, the seven of us, supported by the intercessors across the valley, proclaimed that the victory of the cross would prevail over this high place of demonic habitation.

Time and again in the Books of Chronicles and Kings, the kings are judged to be righteous or wicked depending upon their attitudes toward the high places of idolatry. Although they may have reigned for decades, and may have done many other things, their lives are summarized by whether or not they removed the high places. Of all the kings, Josiah was the most zealous and thorough in removing these altars of idolatry.

> *Josiah brought all the priests from the towns of Judah and desecrated the high places, from Geba to Beersheba, where the priests had burned incense* (2 Kings 23:8).

> *Just as he had done at Bethel, Josiah removed and defiled all the shrines at the high places that the kings of Israel had built in the towns of Samaria that had provoked the Lord to anger* (2 Kings 23:19).

The day we prayed at the Rosicrucian temple was my son Josiah's birthday. Coincidence? I don't think so! (The Scripture that records Josiah being made king is in...you guessed it, Second Kings 22!)

After an hour of prayer and travail, we received the release of the Holy Spirit that our assignment was complete. As we left the temple property, my eyes were suddenly riveted on a small address plaque that we had not previously seen. I was overwhelmed with emotion and completely taken by surprise. Joy exploded within me, and trembling with the fear of the Lord overtook me. The address of that foul place was 2222 Mission Drive! What are the chances of that happening? A street number of 22 or 222 would be an unusual occurrence. But 2222? Again, the Lord was confirming Isaiah 22:22: "I will place on his shoulder the key to the house of David; what he opens no one can shut, and what he shuts no one can open."

The Lord was encouraging us that this place was indeed part of His plan for California, that He was restoring the "mission" of our state, and that the keys of David were being turned to open that which no man can shut...and close that which no man can open. I believe that the day will come when God will remove the prevailing influence of evil from this valley and replace a doorway for the demonic with a portal of Heaven.

When God Opens Heaven

I know God was leading us to "prepare the way of the Lord" through our prayer walk along El Camino Real in 1995. In the short time since that historic pilgrimage, we are hearing encouraging reports that the fires of the Spirit are beginning to burn brighter in the various places where we wept, confessed sin, and prophesied. Surely the King has been welcomed afresh along U.S. Route 101 in California, the wells are being reopened, and the desolate inheritances are being reassigned!

Likewise, our day of intercession at the Rosicrucian temple opened greater access to a visitation from Heaven through our obedience to claim the high places for the Lord. Yet I am convinced there is more. I believe that God wants to show us keys to usher in a day where an atmosphere of an "open Heaven" remains and the reality of God's presence is so thick and so real that believers and unbelievers alike are struck by conviction and awe, and cities and lives are changed forever. I believe that a day of visitation like the revivals of old is coming. David Matthews, speaking on the Welsh Revival, writes:

"A sense of the Lord's Presence was everywhere. It pervaded, nay, it created the spiritual atmosphere. It mattered not where one went the consciousness of the reality and nearness of God followed. Felt, in the Revival gatherings, it was by no means confined to them; it was also felt in the homes, on the streets, in the mines and factories, in the schools, yea, and even in the theatres and drinking-saloons. The strange result was that wherever people gathered became a place of awe, and places of amusement and carousal were practically emptied... The course of the Revival was irresistible. Its reports made up the chief feature in the South Wales daily press for many months. It overshadowed everything else. There was no building large enough to contain the crowds...Within five weeks, 20,000 were added to the churches in South Wales alone. Within eight months, 180,000 were added."[10]

When Heaven is open like this, there is an overpowering awareness of the presence of God, either in a personal experience or in such a powerful way that entire geographic areas are affected by a sense of awe. The results of this open Heaven are witnessed on earth as revival, when large numbers of people seem to fall into the Kingdom, being drawn by an irrestistible hunger. Questions of eternity and salvation seem to be on everyone's mind and preaching becomes nonessential as people just run for the altar.

Oh, that our cities could live this once again! Surely this is what we desperately need...a scattering of the powers and principalities that dominate the minds of millions and a displacing of the atmosphere of evil with the atmosphere of Heaven!

We need to beseech God in prayer for such an open Heaven where He "...would rend the heavens and come down, that the mountains would tremble before [Him]!" (Is. 64:1) Such an atmosphere will not come by trying to build a brick tower of Babel to reach the heavens by the effort of man.[11] The Bible gives us instead an incredible example of having open access to the heavenlies. In Genesis 28, Jacob had "a dream in which he saw a stairway resting on the earth, with its top reaching to heaven, and the angels of God were ascending and descending on it. ... When Jacob awoke from his sleep, he thought, 'Surely the Lord is in this place, and I was not aware of it.' He was afraid and said, 'How awesome is this place. This is none other than the house of God; this is the gate of heaven' " (Gen. 28:12,16-17).

That ladder seemed to bid Jacob heavenly access, much like the open door promised to us in John's vision:

> *These are the words of Him who is holy and true, who holds the key of David. What He opens no one can shut, and what He shuts no one can open. I know your deeds. See, **I have placed before you an open door** that no one can shut. I know that you have little strength, yet you have kept My word and have not denied My name* (Revelation 3:7b-8).

Most people consider this "open door" promised to the Philadelphian church to be an open door for preaching. Yet I believe the Book of Revelation offers us another incredible interpretation:

> *After this I looked, and there before me was a door standing open in heaven. And the voice I had first heard speaking to me like a trumpet said, "Come up here..."* (Revelation 4:1).

This speaks of unhindered access into the heavenlies!

Ezekiel, Stephen, and Peter all saw an open Heaven.[12] Jesus saw an open Heaven at the time of His baptism.[13] The word used here to describe the opening of Heaven literally means "to split or sever (lit. or fig.); to break, divide, open, rend, make a rent."[14] This is the same word used to describe the rending of the temple curtain at the time of Jesus' death, "The curtain of the temple was torn in two from top to bottom" (Mk. 15:38).

God wants His covenant friends to have access to an open Heaven, and to bring that presence here! He wants us to see Him as He is, and to bring that revelation and reality to every place where we are called!

Notice how Jacob experienced an open Heaven. He was sleeping against a stone. Stones often represent covenant in Scripture. Sleeping depicts the most vulnerable and surrendered of positions. Thus Jacob, lying against the "covenant" stone, if you will, was not engineering, controlling, or initiating as the doors of Heaven opened to him. Rather, God moved on behalf of this son of covenant. Resting in complete reliance on the faithfulness of our covenant God and reminding Him of His covenant promises, is the surest way to see this stairway to Heaven established!

We need to contend in prayer and faith for an open Heaven over our cities and an atmosphere where demonic spirits and principalities are banished before the manifest glory and presence of God, and angels are free to ascend and descend. We have not because we ask not!

Ask and it will be given to you; seek and you will find; knock and the door will be opened to you. For everyone who asks receives; he who seeks finds; and to him who knocks, the door will be opened (Matthew 7:7-8).

Surely this promise of a door being opened applies to the door of Heaven! If we have not seen this inescapable, universal sense of the presence of God dominate our cities, if there has been no stairway to Heaven and no dramatic interaction with angelic hosts, it is simply because we have not asked for it!

God wants to show us this door to Heaven and the staircase upon which angels ascend and descend. He is not done with America. He is not done with California. He seeks to open a door into the heavens created not through human effort, but by His gracious invitation, "Come up here."[15] It makes me weep when I think of the humility of Jesus. The resplendent King stands like some stranger off the street, knocking on the door of His own Church, waiting to be invited in: "Here I am! I stand at the door and knock. If anyone hears My voice and opens the door, I will come in and eat with him, and he with Me" (Rev. 3:20). But where is the pastor, the doorkeeper of the house of God, who will take God at His word, recognize Him, and quickly invite Him in? Who will bid Him come?

Oh friends of God, I believe that God wants an open Heaven—it's time to claim the very promise that Jesus Himself spoke to Nathaniel: "You shall see greater things than that...I tell you the truth, you shall see heaven open, and the angels of God ascending and descending on the Son of Man" (Jn. 1:50b-51). I believe that we are entering an hour when God desires to release an unparalled visitation of heavenly host for massive revival—and more importantly, an awesome and overwhelming demonstration of His presence. My heart burns for revival—and for our hearts to cry out in symphony with His: "Rend the Heavens and come down, Lord Jesus! Come quickly!" May we not rest from taking our place before His throne until it is so!

Chapter 7

Claiming Your Inheritance

"About the first of May, a powerful revival broke out in the Lake Avenue M. E. Church in Pasadena. Most of the young men who had come forth in the meetings in Peniel Mission attended this church. They had gotten under the burden for a revival there. In fact, we had been praying for a sweeping revival for Pasadena, and God was answering our prayers. I found a wonderful work of the Spirit going on at Lake Avenue. There was no big preacher there; yet the altar was full of seeking souls. One night nearly every unsaved soul in the house was saved. It was a clean sweep for God. Conviction was mightily upon the people. In two weeks' time two hundred souls knelt at the altar seeking the Lord.... We then began to pray for an outpouring of the Spirit for Los Angeles and the whole of Southern California. ... We are crying, 'Pasadena for God!' Some people are too well satisfied with their own goodness. They have little faith or interest for the salvation of others. God will humble them by passing them by. The Spirit is breathing prayer through us for a mighty, general outpouring.

Great things are coming. We are asking largely, that our joy may be full. God is moving. We are praying for the churches and their pastors. The Lord will visit those willing to yield to Him."[1]

These are the words of Frank Bartleman as he prayed for Pasadena in 1905, speaking of the events that later came to be known as the Azusa Street Revival. The birth of this revival was surely as unlikely and as humble as was the birth of Jesus. Begun in a predominantly black part of town, the revival meetings were held in a barn with dirt floors—a church that had become so neglected that it was used as a stable. William Seymour, a one-eyed black preacher from Houston, Texas, who had come to Los Angeles to preach at a Holiness church, led the first meetings. When the church he had come to serve rejected him because he preached the baptism of the Holy Spirit—a gift he had not yet received himself—Seymour began to hold meetings in a home on Bonnie Brae Street. Being a man of great humility, courage, perseverance, and faith, he gave the Holy Spirit complete freedom in these meetings. (Despite having lost one eye, Seymour was true to his name, seeing more than most men do with both eyes!)

Speaking in tongues characterized this movement and was both sensational and controversial. Even more remarkable, however, was the racial diversity that made up the early core of the revival, being, as Frank Bartleman described it, "some colored, some white."[2] At a time when America was segregated and racial tensions were very real, the power of the Holy Spirit to transform hearts was clearly demonstrated in rich and poor alike. Africans, Native Americans, Latinos, Anglos, Asians—all who were hungry came. Despite pressure from his mentor, Charles Parham, Seymour refused to segregate the races, saying that there needed to be a great coming together in the Church, as at Pentecost, beyond the barriers of race, color, gender, nation, class, or status, to demonstrate that God is no respecter of persons and that all believers are truly one in Christ.[3]

Now there were staying in Jerusalem God-fearing Jews from every nation under heaven. ...each one heard them speaking in his own language (Acts 2:5-6).

The unity that transcended cultural traditions, racial barriers, and social prejudices at Azusa Street is desperately needed today in Los Angeles. By the end of the century, this city will have become the most diverse and international community in the history of mankind. Never before have so many different languages, nationalities, and races lived together! Yet sadly, the memory of the racial harmony at Azusa Street is often overshadowed by Los Angeles' more recent history of racial strife and inequity.

We must reclaim our inheritance. Rick Joyner gave insight into that inheritance as he wrote in the *MorningStar Journal*:

"...the very name *Azusa* was derived from an Indian word that means 'blessed miracle.' This was first noted by Father Juan Crespi in 1769... At the time, *Azusa* referred to the site of an old Indian village...in the San Gabriel Canyon. There, a young Indian girl named Coma Lee used to pray and fast for the healing of her people. ... After she prayed for a chief who was wonderfully healed, he gave her the name Azusa to commemorate his miracle of healing. For many years, Azusa continued her healing ministry while her fame spread all over southern California. During that time whenever there was suffering, people said, 'Go to Azusa and be healed...go to Azusa.' Maybe it is time for us to again go to Azusa and be healed of the many wounds that we have inflicted upon one another."[4]

Establishing a Revival Core

America needs people like Coma Lee, who fasted and prayed for the healing of her people. We need intercessors who set themselves as watchmen upon the walls of their cities, praying day and night, repenting for the sins of their cities, reminding God of His covenants, and giving Him no rest until He again establishes their cities as a praise on the earth.[5] These watchmen are the affection of God's heart, the hope of the city, and a terror to the spirits of darkness. In the words of Mario Murillo,

"The very first stage of revival is to establish a core. Every city needs a group that will set itself aside as a living sacrifice....

"Jesus' voice thunders across the centuries, 'If any two of you agree as touching anything...' (Matthew 18:19 KJV), The promise is that it will be done!...

"There is no prayer that can be prayed that will bring dread upon Lucifer like our prayer made into a revival core. A revival core with the conviction, 'God is going to give us this city!' The road ahead is fraught with many battles and only the truly persistent will survive. We are asking to become the literal altar upon which the fire will fall. You are enlisting in the service of God's retribution on satanic activity in your community."[6]

Several years after I read *Azusa Street*—Frank Bartleman's book about the revival that engulfed the Pasadena area—and cried out to the Lord that Bartleman's mantle of prayer would fall on me, I began to hear stirrings of others who were receiving a similar mandate for Pasadena. Peter Wagner, in particular, drew my attention when he began to form an organization called "Pasadena for Christ," words very similar to the cry of Bartleman decades before. In the infancy of the organization, I was asked to join the intercessory team for Wagner's ministry.

The night before I had to give my answer regarding this invitation, I received a call from Chris Berglund, my covenant friend. Chris called me to tell me that he had seen me in a dream hovering over the city of Pasadena, and he had heard a voice from the Lord say, "Tell Lou that he has an extraordinary gift of intercession for his city."

What a confirmation! I immediately gave myself to the intercession team. Several months later, due to a variety of circumstances, all the other members of the team had resigned, and I alone was left. I will never forget the day when Peter

Wagner laid his hands on me and commissioned me into the intercessory leadership of Pasadena for Christ.

For three years I met with a band of fiery souls who fasted and prayed for our inheritance in Pasadena. In an article for our newsletter, "The Intercessor," I encouraged them with the following words: "Now, I know that you, too, have sensed this appointment to pray for this city, or for some specific sector of it, whether in church, school, business, etc. God has put His finger on your hearts and has quietly nudged you, 'It's time to pray.' " Then I encouraged them with the words of Isaiah 62, admonishing them to stand as watchmen on the walls of Pasadena, and with the memory of Gideon's army of 300, asking them to "form upper room prayer meetings and literally fill the heavenly atmosphere over Pasadena with a ceaseless barrage of prayer artillery."

Men and women of God, in this hour we must proclaim what is our inheritance and set to work to reclaim it. Some of you have undoubtedly shared in groups similar to that of which I am a part in Pasadena. You are hungry for God and eager to see the release of His power in your city. You may, in fact, have been praying for many years.

Be encouraged! In this season of Jubilee, God invites us to ask with great faith:

Which of you, if his son asks for bread, will give him a stone? Or if he asks for a fish, will give him a snake? If you, then, though you are evil, know how to give good gifts to your children, how much more will your Father in heaven give good gifts to those who ask Him! (Matthew 7:9-11)

Sustained By the Promise of Inheritance

The story of Jabez reveals God's response when His people cry to Him with holy ambition and great territorial longing. The account of this man who receives the accolades of Heaven and the distinction of being written into God's book of memories is

placed in the middle of a plain and somewhat boring genealogy: "Jabez was more honorable than his brothers. His mother
had named him Jabez, saying, 'I gave birth to him in pain' "
(1 Chron. 4:9). The name *Jabez* sounds like the Hebrew word
for "pain," but instead of living in self-pity, Jabez fervently
seeks the Lord: "Jabez cried out to the God of Israel, 'Oh, that
You would bless me and enlarge my territory! Let Your hand
be with me, and keep me from harm so that I will be free from
pain' " (1 Chron. 4:10). This one prayer that shows his refusal
to be dominated by pain is all we know about this man. Instead
of dwelling on his pain, he asks for land. Like my heart cry,
"Pasadena for Christ!" he adjures God for a territorial inheritance. So greatly did his prayer please the Lord, that God
answered his request and pronounced him to be "more honorable than his brothers."

Where is your field? What is your inheritance? Of which
spiritual tribe are you a part? As John Dawson says, "Just like
the Old Testament tribes, your movement has a corporate past,
present and future. Your part of God's family has a gift, a
promise and a territory to take."[7] Whatever your inheritance,
God wants to give it to you! His heart beats with a territorial
passion. The earth is the Lord's, and God always gives land
and territories as part of the covenant promises. To be landless
and without territory is to be cursed like Cain: "Today you are
driving me from the land…I will be a restless wanderer on the
earth…" (Gen. 4:14). It is not to be so among us!

Many in the Church have a poor orphan beggar mentality.
We approach God's throne of grace with timidity, cowed by
unbelief and expecting very little. We must get rid of this posture! It is the Father's good pleasure to give us the Kingdom. We
are chosen and destined to fulfill His purposes for our cities!
Only when we free ourselves from this attitude and choose to
approach His throne of grace with bold confidence, relentless
persistence, and a positive expectation of the future will we see
His presence envelop our towns, cities, and country.

Perhaps you are fearful of asking for your inheritance because you don't want to follow in the footsteps of the younger prodigal brother who asked his father for his inheritance.[8] Be assured that the sin of the prodigal son was not in desiring his inheritance, but in wanting it more than a relationship with his father and in using it to escape from his father and from dependency on him.

The Field the Lord Has Given You

God's delight is both to promise His children an inheritance and to give it to them. He is pleased with those who trust Him to give them what is already theirs. This was what set Joshua and Caleb apart from the other spies whom Moses sent to check out the Promised Land:

The land we passed through and explored is exceedingly good. If the Lord is pleased with us, He will lead us into that land, a land flowing with milk and honey, and will give it to us (Numbers 14:7b-8).

When the children of Israel believed the report of the ten spies and refused to go into the Promised Land, God caused them to wander in the desert for 40 years. While all the others of their generation died, Caleb and Joshua thrived. What was it that kept them alone from their generation alive? Surely it was the covenant promise of God that they would receive the very land on which they had walked 40 years before!

You know what the Lord said to Moses...about you and me. I was forty years old when Moses...sent me from Kadesh Barnea to explore the land. And I brought him back a report according to my convictions, but my brothers who went up with me made the hearts of the people melt with fear. I, however, followed the Lord my God wholeheartedly. So on that day Moses swore to me, "The land on which your feet have walked will be your inheritance and that of your children forever, because you have followed the Lord my God wholeheartedly" (Joshua 14:6b-9).

Notice Caleb's boldness in claiming the inheritance that God through Moses had promised him. First he reminds Joshua of God's sworn promise made some 40 years ago—a promise that he fully expects to be fulfilled for him, for his children, and for their children. What faith! Caleb knows that God is bound by covenant to give him his inheritance, so God's covenant promise becomes the basis of his appeal.

Second, Caleb reminds Joshua exactly what his inheritance is to be: "Now then, just as the Lord promised, He has kept me alive for forty-five years....So here I am today, eighty-five years old! ... Now give me this hill country that the Lord promised me that day..." (Josh. 14:10,12). It's more than 45 years since Caleb received the promise, but it is as fresh to him as the day it was given! He knows the boundaries of what he was promised. He is specific. "Give me this hill country," he says.

Third, Caleb recognizes that the timing is right for the fulfillment of the promise. It's his Year of Jubilee. So he asks for his inheritance "now"—and he receives it: "Then Joshua blessed Caleb...and gave him Hebron as his inheritance. So Hebron has belonged to Caleb...because he followed the Lord, the God of Israel, wholeheartedly" (Josh. 14:13-14). Then Caleb goes to war against the demonic powers; binds Arba, the strongman of the Anakites; and takes the Kiriath (field) of Arba and renames it Hebron, which means "fellowship."

When I moved my family right next door to Mott Auditorium, I sensed God say to me, "This land is your Hebron." That morning when I went to church, a friend, Anthon Davis, walked up to me and said, "Lou, this is your Hebron!" Yes! Mott Auditorium was to become my place of communion, my place of covenant fellowship.

God also has a Hebron for you. He has called you to a mission field. If your field seems dry and unproductive, take courage. That is all the more reason to ask the Father for springs of water! Follow the example of Caleb's daughter, who takes the same aggressive posture of territorial prayer as did her father, requesting not only the field but also springs with which to irrigate the field:

> *One day when she came to Othniel, she urged him to ask her father for a field. When she got off her donkey, Caleb asked her, "What can I do for you?" She replied, "Do me a special favor. Since you have given me land in the Negev, give me also springs of water." So Caleb gave her the upper and lower springs* (Joshua 15:18-19).

The promise of God is no trivial thing. It keeps you alive when men are dying all around you. For six years I lived next to Mott Auditorium without seeing God's promised rain. This field had been given to me in the spirit, but my cry was to see the water of the Holy Spirit be released. In January 1995, the waters of refreshing poured out and tens of thousands have since drunk from it. This refreshing of the Spirit has been so wonderful here in Pasadena, but I'm not satisfied. I want both the upper and the lower springs. I thirst for God to give me not just a pool, but the early and the latter rains!

Find the field God has given you. If you don't know where it is, ask Him to reveal this to you. Then like Caleb and the apostle Paul, who recognized the specific field to which he had been assigned, mark out your boundaries and stay within them. To go beyond them is to be presumptuous.

> *We, however, will not boast beyond proper limits, but will confine our boasting to the field God has assigned to us.... We are not going too far in our boasting, as would be the case if we had not come to you, for we did get as far as you with the gospel of Christ. Neither do we go beyond our limits by boasting of work done by others. Our hope is that, as your faith continues to grow, our area of activity among you will greatly expand....For we do not want to boast about work already done in another man's territory* (2 Corinthians 10:13-16).

Paul confined his boasting to his assigned field, but his hope was that his area of activity would greatly expand. He dreamed of going where no man had gone before.

This is the passion of God, the true apostolic vision. He has assigned men and women to fields in every city and every nation, and among people of every race, tribe, and tongue until the shout rings out in truth, "The earth is the Lord's, and everything in it..." (Ps. 24:1)! Be zealous to find your field. Then seize it as your inheritance forever, even when the field seems dry and barren. Fast and pray over it until God pours out His Spirit and the refreshing rains come. He who sets you in the field is faithful and true to bring to pass all that He promises.

The Opening of an Old Well

We are beginning to see this in Los Angeles. The following article on Azusa Street by a well-respected journalist appeared in the *Los Angeles Times* while we were writing this book! It gives some encouraging news about the rebirth of this old well. The writer candidly describes his encounter with these "Pentecostals."

> "I kneel on clean, soft, gray carpet, steadying my suddenly wobbly body by holding onto the pew in front of me. There is another force that keeps me from falling, a slightly trembling hand on my back.... It is the hand of Brother Arturo of Guadalajara. An usher at the church, he's my spiritual sponsor this Sunday afternoon...where aging Chicano gangsters, recently arrived immigrants and poor, hard-working people employed at local factories and in the desert fields live.

> "If you want a religious experience that feels like the raucous times we live in, the Pentecostals can provide it. About 400 million other people around the world have thought similarly and, unlike me, switched from Catholicism or whatever 'mainline' church they grew up with. Pentecostalism is the religion of our times. It has the right tone (apocalyptic), the right rhythm (fast), the right

philosophy (communitarianism as a salve for urban fragmentation and paranoia). You might say Pentecostalism is the MTV of religions: It's hip, precisely what a crew of Pentecostal teens, dressed in torn jeans and flannel shirts, told me at a mammoth Mexico City revival recently: 'We like it because it's *different*.'

"On April 9, 1906, in a wood-frame house on Bonnie Brae Street (in a neighborhood that is today Pico-Union) a new Day of Pentecost came to pass. Over time, the flock who gathered on Bonnie Brae and, later, at a former livery stable on Azusa Street in downtown became famous for causing a quake that rocked the spiritual Richter scale. The Pentecostal gathering featured all the trappings of early Christianity, particularly the mystical, and sometimes downright scary, 'speaking in tongues.' It also was a manifestly L.A. experience, for the City of Angels has always been a place where, despite its radical individualism, and race and class segregation, people, at key moments, always find a way to come together and rise above it all.

"Among the first followers of preacher William Joseph Seymour, an African American, were blacks, whites and Mexicans. What they had in common was that they were all of modest means, the 'forgotten ones' whom the mainline churches had gradually and ultimately neglected.

"*Nearly a century later, on the cusp of the millennium and with not a little millennialism in the air, Los Angeles is on its way to fulfilling the promise of Azusa Street.* Along the Echo Park/Silver Lake corridor of Sunset Boulevard, dozens of storefronts were boarded up as the neighborhood underwent a downturn in the 1980s. Today, cruise Sunset between Alvarado and Fountain and you'll witness a revival that would have made Sister Aimee Semple McPherson proud. (The Pentecostal church she founded, recently refurbished, stands a block below Sunset in Echo

Park, and would be a quiet place today without its Asian, East European and Latin American immigrant following.) 'How many times I prayed to the Virgin of Guadalupe for my husband to stop drinking, for more money to buy the things we needed,' a Latina mother told me recently at a revival meeting in Los Angeles. 'But it only happened when we started going to the Iglesia Cristiana.'

"The Pentecostal revival can be seen as a democratic re-sacrilization of life in the famously hedonistic City of Angels. What has yet to occur is the kind of Pentecost that, as at Bonnie Brae and Azusa Streets, would heal L.A.'s modern-day Tower of Babel and bring rich and poor, white and nonwhite together. At the turn of the century, the tongues spoken by the faithful were radically different, but united in the Spirit (or, in more secular terms, by their common interest in a better world, here and now). But there is faith among the immigrants that just such a day is coming soon."[9]

Praise God! What an incredible prophetic word for our day! It thrills my heart with hope! May you too find your streams of encouragement in the midst of the desert and may we each possess our inheritance so that the earth may indeed "be filled with the knowledge of the glory of the Lord, as the waters cover the sea" (Hab. 2:14).

"Ask of Me, and I will make the nations your inheritance, the ends of the earth your possession" (Ps. 2:8). We ask, Father, as the representatives of Your Son here on earth. Hear our prayers.

Mighty God, possessor of Heaven and earth, we join with the prayers of Your Son. Give us the nations of the world as our inheritance and the ends of the earth as our possession. Lord, give us Pasadena; give us Los Angeles; give us every congregation, neighborhood, city, and nation where You have planted Your servants to reap the harvest. Give Your Church its inheritance of the cities of the earth.

We refuse the counsel of despair. We trust You and believe Your Word, which assures us that all the earth shall worship at the throne of the King. We proclaim Your promise that every tribe and every tongue will come before You in worship, and call it into being. Raise up Your people, O God. Send forth missionaries into the world. Give them their fields and let them possess them for Your sake and for Your glory. Amen.

Chapter 8

Contending for Your Well

Restoring Desolate Inheritances

The Pasadena Nazarene College had moved to San Diego. Erik Stadell was a Swedish missionary who lived in one of the houses on the college campus. Now that the campus was vacant, the Lord put it into Erik's heart to pray fervently that the property would somehow become a mission center.

One day a maintenance worker saw Stadell standing outside the prayer chapel and offered to unlock it so that he could pray inside. Erik recalled, "I went in and a burden of prayer came over me. I prayed all day and into the night. My wife sent my children looking for me, but I told them that I couldn't leave—not yet. I prayed there for a week before the Lord let me leave."[1] In the days that followed, Erik continued to circle the campus in prayer, claiming it for the cause of missions. He cried out to God a covenantal promise, saying, "Before the face of the Lord our God we both speak and confess that the campus of Pasadena College is consecrated for world missions, and can never belong to any other purpose."[2]

Erik had met Dr. Ralph Winter, one of his professors at the Fuller School of World Mission, and they had become good friends. Dr. Winter was also burdened with prayer for the establishment of a major mission center that would lead the way on the global front toward a new, final outreach to the nationalities and peoples as yet unattended by any mission agency, those called "Unreached Peoples." When Winter spoke at Lausanne International Congress on World Evangelization in 1974, he pointed out that 2.5 billion people in the world were still unreached and had no culturally sensitive witness among them. He formed a discussion group to scout out the possibility of establishing a major mission center that would mobilize churches and mission agencies to do something about this need. By early 1976, these plans were mature and the property Erik had been praying for seemed to be the best place.

This place was dedicated to the glory of God! Just after the turn of the century, a group of godly ministers and laymen who wanted to train young men and women for the ministry had acquired the property, and it became the Nazarene College. A great and godly inheritance rested in the place. In fact, all the surrounding streets in the neighborhood are named after the places and people that experienced historic revivals—such as Wesley, Whitefield, Asbury, and Bresee Avenues!

But the college had moved and needed to make payments on their new property in San Diego. Though they had received offers from over 100 organizations, by 1976, after more than six years of negotiations, they still had not found a buyer for the Pasadena property. A New Age cult, The Church Universal and Triumphant (also known as Summit Lighthouse) was aggressively pursuing this holy property and had offered a large amount of money for the option to buy. The trustees knew far too much to be happy about this group but were desperate to sell or rent the campus.

With the vision for a strategic mission center burning in his heart, Dr. Winter contacted the Board of Trustees, which was agonizingly split over selling or even renting to the cult. The next day, in a cliff-hanger moment, the board voted to allow the New Age group to rent all but three of the major buildings on the campus for two years, but denied them the option to buy. Within a few days, Dr. Winter's group was allowed to rent a small part of one of the unrented buildings and to begin the long road to raising the millions of dollars needed to buy the entire property.

After the cult took over, the dormitories that had been home to many young people training to become Christian pastors or missionaries were filled with cult members chanting to their ascended masters: St. Germaine, Krishna, Buddha, and other "spirit guides," who frequently gave "dictations" through the reigning medium and leader of the cult, Elizabeth Clare Prophet. An enormous Buddha squatted on the platform where the gospel had once been preached, and the chanting of "I AM" by this group, which believed an odd mix of Buddhism and Hinduism, filled the auditorium and the surrounding streets 24 hours a day. During cult conferences, a mesmerized crowd "channeled energies" where Nazarenes had gathered for their annual camp meetings, with hundreds, perhaps thousands, having knelt in tears at the old-fashioned "mourners' bench," seeking to confess their sins and to be filled with the Holy Spirit. The Nazarenes who still lived in the area were quite distressed by these changes.

At Fuller, Dr. Winter finally came to realize that if this property was to be saved for missions, he and his family would have to step out alone, despite tremendous odds. None of his friends wanted to be blamed for encouraging him into a plan that, were it not to succeed, might destroy both his reputation and his economic ability to survive. So his family and a few young friends began to pray earnestly that if the establishment of a mission center was indeed the Lord's will, God would do miracles!

Through continuous prayer, periodic fasting, and a lot of hard work, these faithful warriors contended for their promised inheritance. Like Gideon, with his lamps and pitchers, they used methods that often seemed ludicrous to outsiders. Even the cult, looking on from across the street, made fun of their "Jericho marches," when for seven Sundays during the hottest time of the year, Dr. Winter and his supporters, with believers from across the city, circled the campus in prayer, prevailing for victory.[3]

After the cult had been expelled, the U.S. Center for World Mission took over the property and while still trying to pay for the campus gradually began to restore it to its covenantal destiny of being dedicated to world missions. They gave the buildings covenantal names that honored great missionary statesmen and women. These names included those of pioneers like Hudson Taylor (groundbreaking missionary to China), Donald McGavran (father of the Church Growth Movement), and Gladys Aylward (a famous missionary to China). This work of restoration, however, took time. Although the initial down payment had been met, the quarterly $250,000 payments left little money for repairs. Indeed, the USCWM had only seven people to manage the entire property. At one point, not a single blade of green grass could be seen anywhere.

The main auditorium, one of the largest auditoriums in Pasadena, was renamed John R. Mott Auditorium (after one of the principal leaders of the Student Volunteer Movement that released thousands of young people into missions).[4] Built in 1946, its outside walls are still engraved with the promises of Jesus, "Blessed are those who hunger and thirst for righteousness, for they will be filled. … Blessed are the pure in heart, for they will see God" (Mt. 5:6,8). At one point, a major truss of the auditorium ruptured and the entire roof could have collapsed at any second. An unexpected gift, received a few days earlier from a wonderful woman in Phoenix, enabled the $96,000 repair that restored the roof. This came only weeks before a very strong earthquake rocked Southern California.

The physical rebuilding of the campus was not the only restoration begun by the U.S. Center for World Mission. On several occasions the USCWM staff and others had to go through all the buildings, especially Mott Auditorium, to break, through prayer, the residual curses that they felt hung over the campus. Thus through much labor, prayer, and financial commitment the U.S. Center for World Mission sought to reclaim this desolate inheritance, including the auditorium, which had once been so defiled by the cult. It took 13 years, but the miracles happened. Although there was only a handful of people working to raise the money needed to buy the campus, the Lord, true to His Word, provided!

People like Jim Johnston (now a pastor with us at Harvest Rock Church) and his flock, The Cornerstone, continued this process of restoration. Meeting in Mott Auditorium prior to our moving there, they too made inroads to reclaim the glory and rebuild the foundation. In 1989, when our church moved into Mott Auditorium, it seemed that God was allowing Ché Ahn, me, and our church family to have a wider entrance and claim further ground.

At that time I had an office above the auditorium. I remember coming early in the morning to my "prayer closet," this huge echoing building with some 2,500 or so empty, dusty seats. Though the building was infrequently used, God's presence was still there! As I prayed, God spoke to my heart: "Move next door. Get close to this building because something's going to happen here." So I moved into a house across the street.

In the days and weeks that followed, God began to give me a vision for Mott Auditorium. This building would again be a place of His dwelling. I had previously received a clear mandate from the Lord: "I will keep you and will make you to be a covenant for the people, to restore the land and to reassign its desolate inheritances" (Is. 49:8b). Now God was calling me, along with others, to do just that—to seek to fulfill the mission destiny of the holy campus that had been consecrated to God all those years before by the founding Nazarenes and the prayers of Erik Stadell and Ralph and Roberta Winter. God wanted us to devote this huge theater as a place of His presence and a well of revival, to reclaim the purpose for which He had ordained it. As Derek Prince writes, "This work of restoration is the purpose of God for His people at this time. The divinely appointed means to accomplish it is prayer and fasting."[5] So the church started to pray and fast.

I received this vision from the Lord six years before renewal broke out in Mott Auditorium in 1995. I had no idea what was coming! But God gave me a promise that there would be a 24-hour house of prayer in this covenant place. He stirred my heart to believe that this unknown building would fulfill its covenantal name of John R. Mott Auditorium, sending thousands of young people into missions. It would also fulfill its Nazarene destiny to be a birthplace of revival. God was bringing to pass His covenantal faithfulness in this place. But God had to encourage me time and again that He would do it.

Territorial Commitment

When our group of 12 had moved from Maryland to Pasadena with great faith and expectancy in 1984, I had been filled with visions of imminent revival. Then the months ground into years and a sense of failure and disillusionment overtook me. Our field of dreams had become a field of nightmares! For years we held early morning prayer meetings, called corporate fasts, and poured ourselves out before the Lord, but nothing much seemed to be happening.

Then we heard of the prophetic revival meetings being held at Anaheim Vineyard Church. Paul Cain and Mike Bickle (senior pastor of Metro Christian Fellowship of Kansas City) were releasing a lightning storm of fervor. Prophetic signs and gifts were exploding. Oh, how it burned me inside to attend those meetings—or to be anywhere but the stagnant place I seemed to be! Everything within me shouted, "It's time to leave

Pasadena and go to Kansas City!" I just wanted God's presence and it didn't seem like He was in the field He'd given us!

One by one, my best friends and comrades in faith began to leave my church and my city. They too were hungry for God. They went to the Vineyard. They went to Kansas City. A deep sense of abandonment filled my heart. I was tired of going to the wells of other cities to be watered. "God, give me water in Pasadena!" was my cry.

One day, Rondi Moore, a prophetic sister, gave me a word that would change my life forever. She said, "You're always looking to drink from other people's wells, but there is a well beneath *your* feet! Dig it!"

One word from Heaven can change a man's destiny. Instead of leaving Pasadena as I had longed to do, I got out my shovel of fasting and morning prayer and kept digging. Many other faithful brothers and sisters joined me. I knew that there was water beneath my feet; I just needed to reach it. It was the well my spiritual forefather Frank Bartleman had dug in 1905. It was the well of the Nazarenes who had built the auditorium. It was the well of Erik Stadell. I didn't know how long I would have to dig, but I was committed to digging. God had promised that Mott Auditorium is the place of my inheritance; it is my birthright.

Well digging is hard work. In 1990 when I was struggling with disappointment as one friend after another left the church, the Lord gave my friend Chris Berglund a word. In a dream, the Lord said, "You [Chris] are going to Kansas City, but tell Lou it's okay. The two of you will be united again." How intimate and loving of God to share this with His sons. God had spoken very clearly to Chris, so he left for Kansas City and I stayed in Pasadena.

Pasadena was dry in those days. There was a famine in my land of promise. But like Isaac, who had to stay in the land in which his family was repeatedly called "strangers,"[6] I had to stay in Pasadena and contend for my inheritance.

Staying in a land of promise during a famine is never popular. Historically, people have flocked to wherever bread could be found most easily—be it Egypt or whatever church might have plenty. But Isaac obeyed God and stayed in the land despite the drought, planted a field, and reaped a hundredfold harvest![7]

When famine is in the land of promise, don't leave it to go to Egypt unless the Lord says to go. Refuse to judge the harvest that is coming by the drought you are enduring! You never know when harvest might be near at hand.

Two weeks after Chris moved to Kansas City, he found himself in the middle of an outpouring of the Spirit among the students he was teaching at Dominion Christian School of the Metro Christian Fellowship of Kansas City. For 40 days he could hardly teach because kids were slain in the Spirit during class, saw visions, and prayed for four or five hours a day. Talk about jealousy! "Why them and not us?" was my complaint before God. I was happy for Chris, but I had prayed with him for years to experience such things. Still God had said, "There's a well beneath your feet. Dig it!"

During those difficult days, Chris called me just when I needed it most and encouraged my heart in the Lord. He had met an old prophet who had seen the glory of God in the aftermath of the Alexander Dowie healing revivals in Zion, Illinois. This humble and precious prophet knew nothing of Chris, let alone Chris' relationship with me. One of the first words this great lover of God shared with Chris was,

"You have a friend who lives on the border of north Pasadena and south Altadena. He [speaking of Lou] *is seeking revival and he knows that the true spirit of revival is about or begins with seeking the face of God and sitting at the feet of Jesus. You have a relationship with this man*

which was born in Heaven! He has a German name and you must hold fast to this relationship. You will be reunited together."

Oh, what encouragement I received from this word! It was a confirmation of my call as a revival intercessor and as a well digger in the land of my inheritance.

How great is the love and mercy of our God! Had I left Pasadena, the territory of my inheritance, in the early 1990's, I would have missed the multiple blessings and inheritances that I have since received and have yet to receive. But God knew my address and He was faithful to encourage me once I made a commitment to stay where He had planted me.

The principle is this: You must make a territorial commitment to the land of your inheritance. If you don't know where it is, ask God to reveal it to you. And if you don't particularly like the place where God has planted you, ask Him to plant His vision for your inheritance in your heart. Otherwise you will never have the confidence or fortitude to stand in a time of famine or opposition.

I'm reminded of the story of a pastor who lived in a town for which he had little vision. Hoping for a better assignment, he lived with his bags packed. One day God told him to settle down—to unpack his bags and buy a burial plot. The challenge was to make a territorial commitment! The minute the pastor submitted to God, a deep love for his field came into his heart and strategic revelation for the town poured in. He had found his land of inheritance!

The Foursquare Gospel Revival Well

In 1995 renewal burst forth in Mott Auditorium. As we shouted, "We've found water!" I had no idea just how deep the well we had opened was. Since January 1, 1995, when the wave of refreshing broke over us, thousands have come through our doors and been saved, healed, set free, and bathed in the Father's love. Many people have received personal visions and have had supernatural encounters with the Lord as they "rested in the Spirit" on the gym floor of the auditorium.

One evening in the winter of 1996, the Spirit came upon me in a special way. Suddenly it was as if I could see Aimee Semple McPherson (the founder of the International Church of the Foursquare Gospel, which was birthed only a few miles away). I began to cry out, "Aimee's coming back! Aimee's coming back!" Bill Bower, who was praying for me, began to say, "I see the four faces of the cherubim." (Neither of us knew that these four faces were the emblems of the Foursquare Gospel Church.) "Yes," I exclaimed, "it's Ezekiel chapter 1. The glory is coming back to the Church."

This encounter was so profound that I immediately began looking for books on Aimee Semple McPherson and the International Church of the Foursquare Gospel. While reading the book *Aimee: Life Story of Aimee Semple McPherson*, I was captured by Aimee's own description of how she had received the term *foursquare*.

"It was...during this revival in Oakland in July, 1922. The great tent was packed, with multitudes standing around its borders, unable to find a seat beneath the bigtop. The Spirit of God was manifest in a wonderful degree. The great audience listened with rapt attention to my message on 'The Vision of Ezekiel.'

"My soul was awed, and my heart a thrill, for the blazing story of that heavenly vision seemed to fill and permeate not only the tabernacle but the whole earth. In the clouds of heaven which folded and unfolded in fiery glory, Ezekiel had beheld the Being whose glory no mortal can describe. As he gazed upon the marvelous revelation of the Omnipotent One, he perceived four faces, those of a man, a lion, an ox, and an eagle.

"In the face of the lion, we behold that of the mighty baptizer with the Holy Ghost and fire. The face of the ox typifies the great burden-bearer, who himself took our infirmities and carried our sicknesses, who in his boundless love and divine provision has met our every need. In the face of the eagle, we see reflected soul-enrapturing visions of the coming King, whose pinions soon will cleave the shining heavens, whose voice will vibrate through the universe in thrilling cadences of resurrection power as he comes to catch his waiting bride away. And in the face of the man we behold the Savior, the man of sorrows, acquainted with grief, dying upon the tree for our sins. Here is the perfect gospel, a complete gospel, for body, for soul, for spirit, and for eternity, a gospel facing squarely in every direction.

"The whole tent was enveloped as I developed this exposition of God's Word. It was as though every soul there was aquiver with the harmony of celestial music. In my soul was born a melody that seemed to strike and be sustained upon four full quivering strings, as I thought upon the vision of the prophet Ezekiel. I stood still for a moment and listened, gripping the pulpit, almost shaking with wonder and joy. Then there burst from the white heat of my heart the words, 'Why—why, it's the Foursquare Gospel!...' Instantly the Spirit bore witness. Waves, billows, oceans of praises rocked the audience, which was borne aloft on the rushing winds of Holy Ghost revival.

"Since that day when the Lord gave me that illumination, the term *Foursquare Gospel* has been carried around the world, as vividly and fittingly distinguishing the message he had commissioned me to preach of Jesus the Savior, Jesus the Baptizer with the Holy Spirit, Jesus the Healer, and Jesus the Coming King."[8]

I was stunned by the coincidence. What Bill Bower and I had seen on the floor at Mott Auditorium and what Aimee had seen in Oakland in 1922 were almost the same vision.

That same weekend I took intercessors to Angeles Temple, the great Foursquare auditorium in Echo Park in Los Angeles. Nestled next to a beautiful lake, this shining white-domed sanctuary had once been filled nightly with thousands who were seeking healing, salvation, and the baptism of the Holy Spirit. Sustained 24-hour day and night prayer had permeated the place and envoys from Hollywood had come to the Temple to learn Aimee's ways of creative drama. Church planters had been taught and sent out, the sick had been healed, and the poor had been fed. Aimee had shaken Los Angeles for God.

This apostolic well burst out in L.A. just 13 years after Azusa Street. Albie Pearson, a famous baseball player who played a pivotal role in the Jesus Movement, told me of his childhood days in the Temple. Pearson remembers sitting, at age five, through hours of spontaneous, Heaven-directed worship in the Spirit. People were carried along by the heavenly music. Suddenly Albie's mother leaned over and said, "Albie, listen!" Angels could be heard overhead, joining the throngs on earth in their praise of God. Then Albie saw something that was truly amazing: Suddenly, many people who were bound to crutches, braces, and wheelchairs leapt up and were instantaneously healed. A woman with a goiter on her neck the size of a grape-fruit was sitting nearby. Immediately, it fell off before Albie's eyes! What glory, what power!

Gary Goodell, the pastor of the San Diego Vineyard Fellowship, whose father used to usher Aimee up to the stage at the Angeles Temple during his days at Bible college, reports that a Foursquare church is planted somewhere in the world every four hours. There are Foursquare churches around the world. And while there is a wonderful multi-ethnic work going at the original Angeles Temple, the revival glory and harvest of souls known in its founding days are not so evident. The crutches and braces of people who were instantly healed are still displayed inside the building, but the miracles, signs, and wonders that freed them are not the flood they once were. I speak this not to condemn, but to challenge the heirs of the Foursquare glory to redig their wells and reclaim their Pentecostal inheritance!

As the group I had taken to Angeles Temple knelt in that sacred place, we called upon God to redig the well of revival that had burst out there in the 1920's and 30's. My heart is still consumed by our prayers that day. "Oh, God, may Your glory no longer be displayed in memorial cases or hidden in dusty records in the archives. Let Your glory be known. I want to see the glory of God. I want my kids to see it like five-year-old Albie did."

At the time of my vision of Ezekiel chapter 1, I had been invited to speak at a church in Dinuba, California. I knew nothing about the congregation, but I felt led to accept their invitation. I was blown away when a friend called me from Canada and spoke of Steve Witmer, a pastor from Dinuba, California. This pastor, according to my friend, was burdened to redig the wells of the Foursquare glory. The name of his church was Wellspring. Suddenly it dawned on me that this was the church I was to speak at in January. I knew then that I was on a prophetic roll because God had been stirring in me to preach on the theme, "Redigging the Wells of the Foursquare Gospel."

When I called Steve Witmer, he explained how he had gone to a prophetic conference at Wes Campbell's church in Kelowna, British Columbia. At the conference, Jim Goll had told of his prophetic encounters in the Angeles Temple two years before. Steve described for me his experience with Jim:

> "Jim told us how he and several other intercessors had gone to Angeles Temple to pray. As he lay on the platform in the auditorium praying, the pulpit—Aimee's original pulpit built to disappear beneath the stage—suddenly lifted up. Jim became suspended on that rising pulpit. In

that moment, a mighty spirit of prophecy came upon him and he prophesied for 45 minutes concerning the return of the Foursquare glory. In Canada, when Jim shared this story again and reached the point of telling about the prophecy God had led him to release over the Foursquare church, I and two of my fellow Foursquare pastors were picked up by the Spirit and thrown to the floor (I was tossed 10-12 feet) all the while wailing in deep interces- sion. That essentially stopped the teaching portion of that meeting, and it turned to prophetic intercession for the Foursquare to lead the charge in revival and to confirma- tion that we would have a part in redigging these wells of the Foursquare church."

I could hardly believe my ears. "Steve," I exclaimed. "I was there with Jim Goll that day Aimee's pulpit rose and he proph- esied at Angeles Temple."

Oh, what holy coincidences! When I went to the Wellspring Foursquare Church in January 1997, I preached to the young kids, telling them to reclaim their ancient inheri- tances and to redig the well of revival of Aimee Semple McPherson. The Spirit of God wonderfully touched the kids, and the leaders of the church draped a Foursquare flag over my shoulders, adopting me into the Foursquare inheritance.

Early in 1998 I had one divine encounter after another with Foursquare pastors and leaders because of the inheritance I received that day. Without even knowing my prophetic journey of reopening revival wells, they began to speak of the Foursquare Gospel well being reopened and released!

Bethel or Beth Hell?

Many of God's assigned inheritances lie deserted, or they have been overrun by the enemy. I discovered one such place in 1993. Prompted by the Lord, I visited Upland College, a Brethren in Christ campus of which I had fond memories from my youth. What I found horrified me, being in stark contrast to the camp meetings and holiness revival gatherings I vividly remembered attending there as a boy.

The campus had been taken over by Astara, a New Age cult. The place was in disrepair and several buildings were quite run down. Worse than the neglected facilities, however, was the spiritual condition of the place. Occult bookstores filled the buildings where the wells of revival had once flowed. As I walked the campus, I was filled with grief. Here was another desolate inheritance. Standing at the New Age altar, I declared that this place would once again become the house of the Lord.

Soon after my visit to Upland, I spoke at a Brethren in Christ men's retreat and challenged the men to reclaim the former college campus in prayer, proclaiming that when they did reclaim the campus, it would be a sign of coming revival. The Spirit of God stirred those men to pray. One year later I heard that the Brethren in Christ Church had been strongly moved to buy back the campus. In early 1998, I preached on the "Coming Great Worldwide Revival" in that very gymnasium where demons had been worshiped but a few years before.

It seems that geographic locations, not just people or their cultures, have their own spiritual histories that mark them in the spirit realm, predisposing them toward either darkness or light. The sites of sacrifice and covenant, in particular, be they with powers of darkness or with the Lord, seem to have the most spiritual activity associated with them. Effects of godly consecration or demonic defilement seem to linger, influencing the destiny of a place until it is reversed. One of the most striking examples of this phenomenon is the ancient biblical site of Bethel.

The name *Bethel* means "house of God." Located at the intersection of the main north-south road through the hill country, Bethel became important for both geographic and religious reasons. Because of its abundant springs, the area was fertile and attractive to settlers. When Abraham first entered

Canaan, he built an altar at Bethel. Later he returned there to live for a while. These early acts of consecration by God's covenant friend seemed to mark Bethel in the spiritual realm.

It was at Bethel that Jacob saw the Lord, standing at the top of a stairway that stretched from earth to Heaven, and received the promise of the covenant that God had made with his forefathers.[9] It was at Bethel that the ark of the covenant was kept during the time of the judges.[10] It was at Bethel that Deborah, Samuel, and other judges and prophets held court and prophesied.[11]

After the death of King Solomon, when the kingdom was split in two, Jeroboam, the first king of the northern kingdom of Israel, created an idolatrous alternative to the temple in Jerusalem. He built an altar at Bethel, appointed non-Levitic priests, and proclaimed an illegitimate feast.[12] Jeroboam's grasp at spiritual power and control polluted a nation and made Bethel a center of idolatry for nearly 250 years! The devastating summary for the lives of at least ten of Israel's kings is that they "did not turn away from the sins of Jeroboam son of Nebat."[13] Thus a place once holy to the Lord became so detestable and defiled that the prophets Jeremiah and Amos condemned the site and the prophet Hosea called it Beth Aven, meaning "house of idols."[14]

In spite of Bethel's tragic transformation, God was not finished with this holy place. He remembered Abraham and Jacob, and the covenants He had made with them at Bethel. He recalled His plan for Bethel to be a place where His presence was pleased to dwell. So God promised through a remarkably specific prophetic word, 300 years earlier, to send a king named Josiah who would reverse the spiritual curse that Jeroboam had begun. Josiah fulfilled his prophetic destiny by destroying the high places in Samaria, including the altar at Bethel, and by purging both the northern and southern kingdoms of idolatry. The desolate inheritance was restored!

Desolate inheritances like Bethel abound in our land. These places marked by covenant and visited by God's revival fire and water have often been forgotten or overrun by the enemy. But God is not willing to abandon a place once He has visited it! He is jealous for these sites of consecration and sacrifice and will go to great lengths to restore them. Every place God has visited in the past can become a present-day revival well, bringing salvation and refreshing to all who drink from it.

One of these desolate inheritances may be on your street or in your town. Study the moves of God in your area and identify the places He has visited. What is happening there now? Are they abandoned? Have they been overrun by a cult or are they being used for some purpose other than the glory of God? Has Bethel become Beth Aven under your nose? God's counting on you to renew the covenants of your spiritual forefathers, to rebuild the ancient ruins, and to reclaim their prophetic destinies.

Taking Your Stand

Every child of God has some land of inheritance. It may simply be your marriage or your home. It doesn't matter how large or small your inheritance is. Just find it! Then make an intercessory stand for it, refusing to abandon your land of promise no matter what dryness or opposition you encounter. If your field of dreams is your family and your marriage, arm yourself with the weapons of God and fight against "the powers of this dark world and against the spiritual forces of evil in the heavenly realms" (Eph 6:12b) that try to steal your inheritance.

For you see, God is not the only one who is jealous for your inheritance. Demonic powers also want your promised land, especially if it has been consecrated to God through sacrifice and covenant. So take a stand for your field of dreams saying: "Devil, you can't have my children. You can't bring division and disrespect into my marriage. You can't bring drugs onto my street or an adult bookstore into my neighborhood. I declare that this land of my inheritance is a house of God's presence."

As a son or daughter of Abraham, the future of your inheritance rests in your hands. God has prophetically assigned this territory to you. So arise as a covenantal intercessor. Take the keys of fasting and prayer that God gives you and beseech Him for the spiritual well-being of the land He has assigned to you.

First, know the scope of your inheritance. God did not give Adam the whole earth to cultivate, only the Garden of Eden. You have a field with boundaries given by the Lord within which you can exercise great authority as the steward of that sphere. Find your inheritance and learn what boundaries God has placed around your promised land. Then make a territorial commitment to stay there and to defend your inheritance no matter what opposition you may encounter.

Opposition comes in many forms. Some are direct and obvious. You know that you are being attacked. Other forms are more indirect and subtle. Whatever the nature of the attack, set your feet to withstand and refuse to bow to the intimidating pressures that oppose you or to the discouragement and boredom that threaten to consume you. You have a vineyard to tend, and you must not allow it to be turned into a cabbage patch!

An Israelite named Naboth took such a stand. He happened to own a vineyard that bordered on King Ahab's palace. Since the king decided that Naboth's vineyard would be a convenient spot for a garden, Ahab said to Naboth,

> ... *"Let me have your vineyard to use for a vegetable garden, since it is close to my palace. In exchange I will give you a better vineyard or, if you prefer, I will pay you whatever it is worth." But Naboth replied, "The Lord forbid that I should give you the inheritance of my fathers"* (1 Kings 21:2-3).

Do you see the deal that Ahab tried to strike with Naboth? He offered Naboth a "better deal" in exchange for his vineyard. Be careful about better deals! A deal that deprives you of your God-given inheritance is no deal at all. It is your death.

The days of continually looking for promotions that yield bigger fields are over. That model promotes a hireling mentality, which prevents God's people from making a territorial commitment to the vineyard where God has planted them.

Naboth rightly refused to sell his birthright. He was linked to his heritage and was not about to give it up. Queen Jezebel was so perturbed by his stand that she was willing to kill because of his simple act of commitment. Using false accusations from disreputable men, she had Naboth murdered.[15] In many ways this arrogant sin was the final nail in the coffin for Jezebel and Ahab.

The spirit of Jezebel will always seek to dispossess and intimidate those who stand for their rightful inheritance. You must be prepared to commit yourself to your inheritance, even to the point of death. This was the experience of Naboth. He made a simple but costly territorial commitment to his fathers' inheritance. It ultimately cost him his life. However, his commitment also spelled the doom of Ahab and Jezebel's reign of idolatry and witchcraft!

Naboth's life was a life laid down. The same was true for Jesus, who "was assigned a grave with the wicked, and ...poured out His life unto death..." (Is. 53:9,12). Theirs was true intercession, for intercession is much more than prayer. Intercession certainly embraces prayer to God, and God may graciously answer, but the root of intercession is death.

Naboth's intercession was not in spoken words. It was in taking a stand in his field. It was in refusing to crumple under the fear of men. It was in his attitude that said, "I will never give you my field. You can have it over my dead body." There is a powerful spiritual warfare principle in this: "Therefore put on the full armor of God, so that when the day of evil comes, you may be able to stand your ground, and after you have done everything, to stand" (Eph. 6:13).

I have close friends who are missionaries among a certain hidden people group. They know that they are called to the city where they minister; they know their inheritance. Sickness, setbacks, isolation, and discouragement challenge them on all sides demanding, "Give me your vineyard!" to which they respond, "The Lord forbid that I give you my fathers' inheritance."

Begin to intercede with faith for your inheritance. If your promised land suffers from abandonment and disrepair, begin to pray in faith for these ruins. Learn how God has poured Himself out there in the past and remind the Lord of these pleasant memories. Recount the sacrifices, the acts of consecration, and the covenants that have been made there. Teach them to your children and share them with your close friends. These things are still fresh in God's memory. They will move His heart until the cup of His Spirit overflows and He revisits your special inheritance.

Then you will be privileged, as I have been, to share in God's restoration program, and the promise of Isaiah will become your commendation: "Your people will rebuild the ancient ruins and will raise up the age-old foundations, you will be called Repairer of Broken Walls, Restorer of Streets with Dwellings" (Is. 58:12). Your territorial stand may also spell the doom of some evil that has held your inheritance in its sway: "The scepter of the wicked will not remain over the land allotted to the righteous" (Ps. 125:3a).

Arise, intercessors of America. Arise, heirs of God. Seek the Lord concerning your inheritance and stand for it unequivocally once you find it. Restore the desolate inheritances of the Bethels in your neighborhood. Then may God's heart be stirred to revisit the places marked by sacrifice and covenant and to affirm your call as an intercessor, a well digger, and a restorer in the land of your inheritance.

Chapter 9

The Arrow of Victory: Prophetic Prayer Assignments

The intricate sand sculpture was finished. Experienced Tibetan monks had spent hundreds of hours building it in preparation for a visit from the Dalai Lama. Accompanied by an entourage of Tibetan monks and high level spirits, he was coming to Pasadena to hold large meetings in the Civic Auditorium. Several well-known Hollywood celebrities were expected to attend. The "blessing" of the sand mandala at the Pacific Asian Museum was to be the highlight of the Dalai Lama's visit. As world leader of the Tibetan branch of Buddhism, the Dalai Lama exerts tremendous spiritual authority. This ceremony was to create a doorway through which 722 powerful spirits could be released into the area surrounding Pasadena!

Harvest Rock Church had already experienced several significant encounters with the spirit of Buddhism. A large Buddha had once occupied center stage in the building that is now our church, placed there by the New Age cult that had occupied the campus. In 1996, with the visit of the Dalai Lama approaching, we gathered the entire church together for worship and spiritual warfare. Many intercessors cried out to God in the prayer room.

We prayed for the salvation of the Dalai Lama and other Buddhists, particularly the many who are employed in Hollywood. A small group of intercessors also went down to the Pacific Asian Museum. This building, located in the center of Pasadena, is right across the street from Fuller Seminary. As the group prayer-walked the museum, they anointed the perimeter of the property and laid hands on the building, sealing it off from demonic forces. At a second prayer walk, several intercessors laid a spiritual ambush at the front door, asking the Holy Spirit to touch the Dalai Lama as he walked through it.

As the day of the Dalai Lama's visit approached, a report was released that although he was going to visit the museum, he would not pray over the mandala after all! Thus Pasadena was to be spared this flood of 722 demonic spirits. Moreover, the sand from this unholy sculpture was not poured into the Arroyo Seco—the river that supplies the Los Angeles area with water—as had been planned, but was put into the sea near Santa Monica, where freak waves were reported for several days. Again, Los Angeles was spared.

A striking change of events also took place at the Civic Auditorium. Camera crews from around the world had gathered on the steps of the Civic Auditorium, hoping to get a few shots of the Dalai Lama with Hollywood celebrities.

Prior to this media event, an intercessor had gone to the building, laid hands on the steps, and prayed that the presence of the Lord would be released there. When the big day arrived, the limousine carrying the Dalai Lama pulled up to the steps. The door opened, then closed again…then opened and closed again. This happened several times, but nobody got out of the car, spoiling this carefully planned media spectacle!

The events surrounding the Dalai Lama's visit certainly encouraged our intercessors. Although the mayor of Pasadena had given the keys of the city to the Dalai Lama, praise God the keys of the Kingdom are in the Church's hands, and if we use them, we can lock out the powers of hell!

Cleansing the Waters

Evidence of the power of prophetic intercession (specific intercession and actions directed by the leading of the Lord) has been shown to me numerous times. One night I was awakened by words that had been spoken to me in a dream: "Go pour the salt of your purity out on it." I knew that the Lord's voice had spoken these words, but I didn't understand then what they meant.

The following morning I went to a prayer meeting, during which Kateri Matilla, an intercessor from our church, prayed that God would change the name of Devil's Gate Dam. Suddenly, it struck me forcefully that the Lord wanted me to go pour salt into the stream at Devil's Gate as an act of prophetic intercession!

Devil's Gate was the name of a dam that protected the original water source for Pasadena and Los Angeles. A 1947 *Star News* article confirms that Devil's Gate was so named "because of the resemblance of the rocks to His Satanic Majesty."[1] Several people were killed during the construction of the freeway near the dam, and numerous murders and suicides have occurred along the river, the Arroyo Seco, that flows from the dam. Intercessors in Los Angeles have sensed that the name literally brought a curse on the city.

As I recalled the words in my dream, I understood that the Lord wanted me to pour salt into the stream as a sign of cleansing, to ask for forgiveness on behalf of our forefathers for cursing the water, and to entreat God to pour out the rivers of revival on Pasadena and Los Angeles. As I contemplated God's command, I was reminded of a Scripture the Lord had impressed upon my heart prior to coming to Pasadena.

The men of the city said to Elisha, "Look, our lord, this town is well situated, as you can see, but the water is bad and the land is unproductive." "Bring me a new bowl," he said, "and put salt in it." So they brought it to him. Then he went out to the spring and threw the salt into it, saying, "This is what the Lord says: 'I have healed this water. Never again will it cause death or make the land unproductive.'" And the water has remained wholesome to this day... (2 Kings 2:19-22).

In this passage, Elisha poured salt into the stream of water that flowed into Jericho, healing the contaminated waters that were unfruitful and barren. God was asking me to do the same for Los Angeles, to bring healing and fruitfulness to the waters that were producing spiritual death.

Shortly after my dream, an intercession team joined me at Devil's Gate, where we poured salt into the stream and called for a renewal of God's covenant mercies. (It seems fitting that God would choose salt for this prophetic gesture because it is a preserving element.) We prophesied a changing of the demonic name and the removal of the curse cast by the giving of the name. We also asked God to forgive the people of Los Angeles for breaking covenant with Him.

At the time of our visit to Devil's Gate, southern California was in the midst of a five-year drought. Many thousands of Christians were praying for rain. Eight days after our intercessory act on behalf of the city, the rains began to pour so much so, that the newspapers hailed that month "Miracle March."

Astonishing! We took courage from this dramatic break in the drought that God was answering our prayers. The curse was being reversed. We also pondered whether this physical rain might not be a sign of coming spiritual renewal.

Some time later I felt drawn by the Spirit to walk the Arroyo Seco, the stream flowing out of the dam (and the main river of Los Angeles), to pray for rivers of revival to flow down again from Pasadena and bring fruitfulness into Los Angeles.

Interestingly, the last meeting of the Azusa Street organization was held in the Arroyo Seco, between Los Angeles and Pasadena. That's where that mighty well of revival had dried up.

As I walked along the river, I was also praying over the whole issue of death and murder in the Arroyo. A year before, a Christian woman whose parents were missionaries to Buddhists was abducted and murdered in the Arroyo. So I interceded by identificational repentance for the spirit of murder to be broken. I also prayed for the redeeming of the land where, during the Depression, people had leaped to their death from Suicide Bridge, a bridge spanning the Arroyo.

Two days after my prayer walk, a sister in the Lord told me that she had dreamt that I was walking the river and interceding in the Arroyo—having no idea that I had done just that! This was great encouragement to me to continue this type of intercession. Some might call these prophetic actions foolish, but God is calling forth a people who will respond to His leading no matter how foolish, irrational, or insignificant His command might seem to be. Time after time, such obedience is recorded in the Word of God.

For two years we saw no visible evidence that our acts of prophetic intercession had accomplished anything more. One day Angela Blair, an intercessor on the team that had gone to the dam, asked the Lord why the name of Devil's Gate had not yet been changed. The Lord answered her that the name was indeed changing, and that in the days ahead the dam and the surrounding area would be called by an Indian name. Imagine our joy when one month later we read this announcement in the "Pasadena Focus," the official city newsletter: "*Hahamongna*. That's the name the Gabrielinos (early Pasadena Indians) gave to what now is known as 'Devil's Gate...'. The English-language translation is 'Flowing Waters: Fruitful Valley.' Nearly everyone agrees that *Hahamongna* will be a more approriate name for this long-neglected community asset after it is restored to its natural state."[2]

The very words we had proclaimed prophetically were now proclaimed publicly! We had specifically prayed that the curse of barrenness would be broken, as it was when Elisha cleansed the water of Jericho. Now the official Pasadena newsletter reported the reinstatement of the original Indian name, Flowing Streams and Fruitful Valley. It was a sign for us that revival would come to Pasadena and flow to Los Angeles.

God has required our team of intercessors to respond in a variety of ways. Generally the intercessory acts He's asked us to perform have been acts of repentance and purification in which we claim, seal, or consecrate a territory, or acts that prefigure something the Lord wants to do. We embark upon these activities *only* by the word of the Lord. If He doesn't speak, we don't go.

I cannot stress enough the need to be completely subject to the Lord in this. Intercessors must never initiate these assignments. They must simply respond when they hear the voice of the Lord and there is confirmation. If these acts are to have an effect on the spiritual realm, and not be merely meaningless antics, they need to be done in faith at the Lord's command, not as impulsive responses to our imaginations. The Lord's commands to us have come in various forms, including scriptural precedent, prophetic dreams, confirmed prophetic words, and symbolic events. Very often they are linked with a spiritual battle to reclaim or protect our land of inheritance.

The Arrow of Faith That Changes History

The Book of Second Kings tells of one such battle. Elisha, who received a double portion of Elijah's mantle and performed miracles and signs in Israel over a period of 60 years, is dying. He has summoned Jehoash, the king of Israel, for one final audience to bless Israel. During the encounter, Elisha tells the king to take some vital prophetic actions.

Elisha said, "Get a bow and some arrows," and he did so. "Take the bow in your hands," he said to the king of Israel.... "Open the east window," he said, and he opened it. "Shoot!" Elisha said, and he shot. "The Lord's arrow of victory, the arrow of victory over Aram!" Elisha declared. "You will completely destroy the Arameans at Aphek" (2 Kings 13:15-17).

Notice that the arrows became "the Lord's arrow of victory" in a very real way. Jehoash's actions, blessed by Elisha, released the power of God on behalf of Israel. This was no empty pantomime, but an act of obedience that affected the destiny of the entire nation! Victory or defeat, survival or slaughter, were determined by this apparently silly action.

Unfortunately, Jehoash was somewhat apathetic about performing this prophetic act. Certainly he must have known the stories of Elisha's command to dig ditches in a deserted valley where soldiers were dying of thirst—and how those ditches were miraculously filled with water.[3] So Elisha gave him another chance to overcome his indifference:

Then he said, "Take the arrows," and the king took them. Elisha told him, "Strike the ground." He struck it three times and stopped. The man of God was angry with him and said, "You should have struck the ground five or six times; then you would have defeated Aram and completely destroyed it. But now you will defeat it only three times" (2 Kings 13:18-19).

Elisha had told Jehoash that his actions would determine the future of the Israelite people, but the king did not truly believe the prophetic word. His wavering cost many Israelite lives, and Israel gained only partial victory. History was changed by a poor and casual response. Had Jehoash believed the impact of his actions, he would have repeatedly smashed the arrows into the ground.

We, too, are given opportunities to prophetically intercede for the land of our inheritance. These opportunities may require us to take a prophetic action that, in the natural, seems to be puny, unrelated, or even foolish. Beware! What appears to be absurd or insignificant in the natural may accomplish great things in the spiritual realm when done in faith and obedience.

Elisha repeatedly proved this to be true. Why else would he have thrown a stick into the water to make a heavy, very valuable axehead float to the surface? Or why put flour in a pot as an antidote to poisoned food? Or why ask for a neighbor's empty vessels to fill when it seemed that only a few drops of oil could be poured into them?[4]

Prophetic action does not need to make sense in the natural to be powerful in the spirit realm. The measure of victory is equal only to the measure of our faith and obedience. These are the keys that empower seemingly ineffective actions. Thus, Tommy Tenney, a group of intercessors, and I took stakes with scriptural promises in them and planted them in the ground on Bonnie Brae Street, the site of the prayer meeting that birthed the great Azusa Street Revival. We did this in obedience to God, believing that our actions would impact the future of our city.

We must arise in faith and obedience, doing whatever God commands us to do. Through our obedience coupled with faith the revival wells stopped up by sin, disunity, curses, and covenant breaking will be reopened. For just as the artesian well of the Holy Spirit within an individual can be stopped up by sin, curses, and bitter root judgments, so can a city be bound by the sin within.

God is raising up prophetic intercessors throughout our land. These committed covenantal friends will walk the boundaries of their homes, churches, and communities to break every stronghold as the Lord leads. They will find the roots that clog the flow of God's Holy Spirit and remove them so that rivers of life and fruitfulness may flow into the parched lives of thousands. This process is happening right now in Hollywood.

Hollywood Jubilee—Revival in Tinseltown?

Hollywood...the city of glitter and lights, the place of dreams that are never fulfilled and would-be stars who never make it big. Can God bring revival to this tinseltown? The archives of history answer a resounding yes! Hidden in this city's past is a great outpouring of the Holy Spirit, a refreshing revival well.

It was the year 1947. Henrietta Mears, a woman of great devotion who spent much time with the Lord, was at that time the leader of the college department at the First Presbyterian Church of Hollywood. She also served the congregation as the Director of Christian Education and wrote the Sunday school curriculum, founding Gospel Light Publishing, now Regal Books.

On June 24, 1947, Mears spoke to hundreds of Sunday school teachers, pastors, and young seminary students.

"She spoke of the totalitarianism that had recently gripped Germany under Hitler and the threat of the spread of communism.... Just as men of special courage had been called upon for difficult assignments during World War II as 'expendables,' so she felt that Christian believers should become expendables for Christ. She emphasized the necessity of revival, prayer, and renewed interest in the Scriptures.

"Among the people who attended this Teacher's Conference were Reverend Richard C. Halverson…Louis H. Evans, Jr., the son of the pastor of the church; John L. Frank; and William R. [Bill] Bright, who had become a Christian only a few months earlier. After Miss Mears' message, these four young men, with several others, asked her if they could meet for prayer in her cabin. Baldwin and Benson, biographers of Henrietta Mears, describe the ensuing prayer meeting:

'As they knelt, they were overcome by a sense of helplessness and inadequacy. They prayed on into the late hours of the night, confessing sin, asking God for guidance, and seeking the reality and power of the Holy Spirit. There was much weeping and crying out to the Lord. At times, no one prayed as God spoke to them.

'Then, the fire fell. However it can be explained, God answered their prayer with a vision. They saw before them the college campuses of the world, teeming with unsaved students, who held in their hands the power to change the world. The college campuses—they were the key to world leadership, to world revival!'

"...The following evening, these five people returned to the Presbyterian church at Hollywood to speak at the weekly Wednesday evening prayer meeting of the college department of the church.

'As Miss Mears entered the room, one of those present said to another, "I have never known before what it meant in the book of Exodus where it describes Moses' face shining with the glory of God, but now I see: Look at Teacher's face!" ' "5

Out of this incredible meeting came forth a vision for the college briefing conferences of the next few years that were held at the Forest Home Conference Center. During the 1947 revival at Forest Home, Bill Bright gave up a secular business to give himself to ministry, later birthing Campus Crusade for Christ. At the 1949 briefing conference, Billy Graham was mightily impacted by the Holy Spirit through the ministry of Dr. J. Edwin Orr and a personal vision God gave him during the same time. Graham then held a great crusade meeting in Los Angeles. Sponsored by Christ for Greater Los Angeles, in cooperation with 1,000 churches of all denominations, the meetings were extended from the three weeks originally planned to eight weeks. The conversions of Stuart Hamblen (a television star), Louis Zampernini (a former Olympic athlete), and "an alleged associate of the notorious racketeer, Mickey Cohen," drew so much attention from the media that 3,000 seats were added to the tent, making available a total of 9,000 seats. Even then thousands who couldn't get inside the tent stood outside.

This outpouring of the Holy Spirit also affected movie stars and other Hollywood celebrities. Colleen Townsend, Roy Rogers, Dale Evans, Tim Spencer, and Connie Haines were among the many Hollywood stars who were converted. In 1949, a few Hollywood film stars met in the cabin of Henrietta Mears to pray for guidance in touching the lives of their friends in the film industry. Subsequent meetings were also held, each being convened in private homes to avoid publicity. From 1949 to 1951, these gatherings were under the direction of J. Edwin Orr, who served as chaplain.

> "The first meetings were immediately successful. Miss Mears' spacious living room was packed with the famous, many scores of whom found the Saviour, and some of whom rejected him."[6]

Cameramen and technicians also became involved in this group, whose talents Billy Graham used to launch his first film crusade.

All this and much more was born out of Hollywood Presbyterian Church as Henrietta Mears, a mother in the faith, dug a well of revival. The flood from this well burst forth and affected the whole world through the wells of crusade evangelism like Billy Graham's, and the campus ministries like Bill Bright's. Even to this day, First Presbyterian Church of Hollywood continues to have a great influence. Lloyd Ogilvie, a former pastor of the church, is now serving as the U.S. Senate chaplain, following in the footsteps of Richard Halverson, who also served as chaplain of the Senate.

Fifty years later, God is again working in Hollywood. In 1996, one of our prophetic intercessors described an intense dream encounter to me. In the dream, this intercessor saw one of the L's in the famous "Hollywood" sign on the hills surrounding the city fly out and go to Mt. Wilson above Pasadena. The sign then became "Holy Wood," and Mt. Wilson became "the Will of the Son."

When I heard this dream, I might have been tempted to laugh and say, "That's what happens when you eat pizza at night before you sleep." But no, I felt strongly that the dream was profound, a prophetic prayer assignment given by God. The day after I was told this dream, I received a phone call from a prayer mobilizer in Washington, D.C., who told me that Cindy Jacobs had just called him and told him to talk with me. He was to tell me about the prayer mobilization that was going to happen in Hollywood. As this prayer warrior was talking with me on the phone, he suddenly said, "And my son told me this morning that God wants to take the L out of Hollywood and make it Holy Wood." Here again, with this confirmation, I knew that this was the word of the Lord.

Soon after this phone call, some of our intercessors, having heard the prophetic word, began to do prayer walks in Hollywood. Sonny Roberts led a prayer walk right down one of the major streets of Hollywood. Our intercessors also began to go into the bars to pray. A wonderful sense of encouragement began to come, and months later, there seemed to be a growing sense of prayer.

Jeri Penley and Rick Clark, who leads a ministry called Pray Pasadena 2000, have also been laboring under a burden of prayer for Hollywood. Having heard my vision for a 24-hour house of prayer, they have begun to unite churches to establish a 24-hour house of continuous prayer for Hollywood in Hollywood.

What's happening in Hollywood is the preparing of ground for a great move of the Lord. He's raising up intercession, prayer, and worship to prepare the way for His coming. One of the intercessors associated with John Dawson at the YWAM base in Los Angeles and I spoke for three hours concerning this wave of intercession that God is raising up for Hollywood. Then we prayed and asked, "God, show us the next step. What would You have us do in our prayers for Hollywood?"

That night I preached at Mott Auditorium. After the meeting, a man walked up to me and shared what he had dreamt the night before. In the dream, he saw my wife. She was pregnant, a mother ready to give birth and to nurse the nations. Her mouth was closed and she couldn't speak because she was so expectant. In the dream, this man told her, "You will nourish many, many children." Suddenly, as he said this, my wife's mouth was opened in the dream and she said, "You must pray with Lou in the basement of Hollywood Presbyterian Church." When this man shared this with me, I knew that the Lord was speaking. He was giving me a prophetic prayer assignment to redig the well of the Hollywood Presbyterian Church through intercession. The symbolism in the dream was that my wife represented the fruitful, spiritual motherhood of Henrietta Mears.

Soon after this occasion, I gathered together 30 intercessors. We went to the basement of Hollywood Presbyterian Church, precisely where Henrietta Mears had held her meetings some 50 years before. We prayed that God would reopen this revival well and that Hollywood Presbyterian Church would once again see a great move of the Holy Spirit.

In 1998, God's call to prophetic intercession has led us literally all around Hollywood to pray. We have stood in front of theaters and have climbed the hills near the Hollywood sign praying that God will open the Hollywood wells once again. Children and adults alike are hearing God's call.

In February, my son Jesse said abruptly, "Dad, the angels are gathering." "What do you mean, Son?" I asked. "I'm reading the book *This Present Darkness* by Frank Peretti," Jesse replied, "in which the angels are doing battle in the heavens. I think it's prophetic for Los Angeles right now."

I was taken aback by his insight, then thought nothing more of it. The following day, I received a surprising phone call. The man on the phone introduced himself saying, "Hello. I'm Bruce Isacson, the producer of a movie called 'This Present Darkness.'" I could hardly believe the coincidence. Mr. Isacson went on to tell me that his life had been changed at Mott Auditorium, and that he felt like he should call me.

In January, just several weeks prior to all this, an intercessor had encouraged me to meet with a Foursquare pastor whose church is in Azusa, California. She felt that our hearts would connect. However, I had been so busy fasting and interceding that I had put it off. As I talked with Bruce Isacson on the phone, he suddenly said, "I feel like you should meet Rick MacDonald, my brother-in-law. He's the pastor of the Foursquare church in Azusa, California." Again I was taken aback. I knew that this had to be a divine appointment.

When I went with my prayer partner Ray Clarke to meet with Rick MacDonald, the spirit of intercession fell on us heavily as Rick shared that his congregation was about to embark on a 21-day fast that would target Hollywood and Azusa. Here was but one more scrap of evidence that God is appointing His intercessors to pray for a Jubilee in Hollywood, and there are others. Tim Storey is leading a major Bible study in Hollywood with packed audiences, and stories of movie stars being awakened continue to reach us. Members of the Hollywood Presbyterian Actors Guild have been praying for an outpouring of God's Spirit, with some having participated in a 40-day fast for the city. They are well diggers.

The redemptive gift of Hollywood for the world is communication. The "City of Angels" was destined by God to be a messenger city. But the devil has done much to pervert this gift. Movies and other media filled with filth have flowed from the city to pollute the world, but the time has come for the reclaiming of Hollywood's apostolic gift. And it is beginning! Christian songs are penetrating major movie productions. Stories are circulating of star conversions. Christian themes are slowly infiltrating top-rated television programs. Movie titles and storylines even prophesy God's soon-coming power.

The devil would say that we cannot approach his citadel of Hollywood. I disagree. The promise given to us through our father Abraham is that we will possess the gates of our enemies. Satan no longer has any safe place that he can use as a stronghold. San Francisco, Hollywood, and Los Angeles can once again be recaptured for the Lord as the Church mobilizes in massive intercession, fasting, and prayer.

The story of Hollywood's revival well and the redigging that is now going on is but one story of what God is doing, and is wanting to do, in cities across our land and around the world. He is raising up houses of prayer for day and night worship and intercession. He wants to start such a house in your city and in your neighborhood. Why? God remembers Henrietta Mears, Billy Graham, and Bill Bright. He remembers the spiritual fathers and mothers who dug a well of revival in your city. He is moved by their devotion and sacrifice and is preparing to send fire once again on their offerings. He wants to release His Holy Spirit as He did in 1948 and 1949, pouring forth the anointing of great evangelists like Billy Graham and Bill Bright.

We are called to be gatekeepers, people who close the door on the demonic and open the door to the Holy Spirit. Each person, congregation, and denomination has received a gift, a territory, and a promise. In Jubilee, we must move to reclaim them.

Recently, after much repentance for the sins committed there, a group of intercessors drove stakes filled with scriptural promises into the ground in Hollywood at various strategic sites, believing that the Lord is again going to powerfully visit this vast, influential industry.

What touches your heart…or to what industry, vocation, or institution can you lay claim? If we are passive about laying claim to our land of inheritance, the enemy will run rampant. But if we claim just one part of our territory and say, "Lord, that's Yours," we may provide a beachhead from which the Lord can launch revival. Start somewhere. When the Lord gives you a prophetic action to take, be obedient and do it in faith, fully expecting Him to respond. Give yourself to seasons of consecrated prayer and fasting, focusing on whatever target the Lord gives. Join with other Christians and pray with unity for your community. As we obey God in these things, the Church can be a powerful demonstration of His love for our families, our communities, our nations, and our world, and of His power to dislodge the principalities of evil that freely spread their influence in our land.

Father God, we ask in the name of Jesus for an outpouring of grace, mercy, and fire. Send Your Holy Spirit to cleanse us, break us, and humble us so that true spiritual revival can come to and cover our cities, causing a turning back to God. We ask that the destiny of Hollywood, Los Angeles, and cities across our land and around the world not be aborted. Visit us, filling our homes, our churches, and our communities with Your glory. Do not pass us by.

We ask for a restoration of the foundations of righteousness for Los Angeles and every other city You have visited in the past. By submission to You, Holy Father, and by faith in Your great love and power, we resist the devil and his works and give notice to all forces and powers of evil that have taken hold of our communities. We oppose the spirit of wickedness and all other demonic spirits that have established strongholds in our cities. We call on the name of Jesus to reveal and destroy all these spiritual strongholds—the dark places, the hidden works of darkness, the mystery sites where the enemy has set up his encampments—and we proclaim this day that the city of Los Angeles (insert name of your city or neighborhood) is now under the power and ownership of the Holy Spirit. All other spirits are hereby given notice and evicted from this property by the power of the name of Jesus. Today we stand in the gap, obedient in prayer and prophetic action, and build a hedge of protection around this city. Amen.

Chapter 10

The Travail of Prophetic Intercession

I will never forget the birth of our son Jacob. My wife, Therese, felt that she was going into labor, so we raced off to the hospital. When the contractions slowed down, we were sent home again. No sooner had we reached home than Therese realized that this was indeed the real thing! So we started to speed back to the hospital, but encountered Los Angeles' famous rush hour traffic and were literally parked on the freeway! Therese kept telling me that the baby was coming, and I kept trying to move through traffic that was barely moving. Once we got to the hospital, Therese gave birth in eight minutes to an eight-pound baby, the eighth member of our family. And yes, the date of birth was the eighth day of the eighth month!

No one knows exactly when a baby will be born. In the first days and weeks after a woman conceives, she does not feel any sign of the life within her. In fact, she may not even know that she is pregnant. But as time goes on, her body begins to change and she endures the morning sickness, leg cramps, backaches, and fatigue that signal the baby's presence. Still she goes about her daily responsibilities, making some adjustments, perhaps, but seeing no major changes in her life. For nine months, as she carries and nourishes the life within, her body gives increasing evidence of the infant she carries, but the child is not yet in sight. Suddenly, without warning, the birth pains start and the woman's body prepares to deliver the child.

Birthing prayer is much like this. At first there is little evidence of the life that God is preparing to pour out. In truth, it may even appear that there is no life. This is the way it was for several years after Ché Ahn and I moved to Pasadena in 1984.

In 1982, God had dramatically called 12 of us to move from Maryland to Los Angeles. When we moved to Pasadena two years later, we fully expected to start reaping the "great harvest" the Lord had promised us. So we rented the Pasadena Civic Center and prepared for this great outpouring of the Lord. Don't do that! When no one showed up, we lost a lot of money!

Chronos and *Kairos* Prayer

The years that followed were certainly not as exciting as we had originally expected them to be. We had the word of the Lord that we would reap a great harvest, so we planted the new church with ten days of fasting and prayer. This was the beginning of ten years of praying for the revival God had promised. I remember some prayer meetings where 60 people gathered every morning at six o'clock and it was just intense. I also remember some times when there were only two of us praying, myself and an elderly lady from another church. Morning after morning intercessors prayed in that freezing, deserted auditorium, wondering why we got up so early and what we were doing there.

This ordinary prayer in dry times is what I call *chronos* prayer—that is, prayer within *chronos* (ordinary) time. It's the day in, day out prayer that seems to have little effect, but in truth is slowly filling the bowls of Heaven. We often have no idea that our prayers are doing anything; but day by day, little by little, we are preparing for the moment of climax, as when a woman gives birth to her baby: "The smoke of the incense, together with the prayers of the saints, went up before God from the angel's hand" (Rev. 8:4).

Kairos prayer, on the other hand, is the travail that brings the special times, the "divine appointments" on God's calendar, to pass: "Then the angel took the censer, filled it with fire from the altar, and hurled it on the earth; and there came peals of thunder, rumblings, flashes of lightning and an earthquake" (Rev. 8:5). These times are characterized by certain climatic events—for example, "the time [*kairos*] of harvest" spoken of in Matthew 13:30 (KJV). What is important here is that much prayer must be presented to the Lord during the *chronos* times before there can be an overflowing into *kairos* events.

As intercessors, we may pray for years in *chronos* tedium before we experience the *kairos* passion of God's great visitations. Let us not lose heart when we do not see immediate results. Christians in the former Soviet Union, for example, prayed through 70 years of patient travail before the Communist regime collapsed. Throughout those years, the spirit powers behind the godless government were increasingly bound by the massive outpouring of tears and prayers that arose from the persecuted Church as a memorial before God. Could the praying Church see the work that was being wrought by their years of prayer? Certainly not! It was only in the *kairos* moment, when the sheer volume of prayer affected Heaven and brought forth an extraordinary season of time, that the results of their many intercessions became visible.

This faithful *chronos* prayer is also evident in the life of Cornelius, a devout, God-fearing Gentile. Acts 10:4 states that Cornelius' prayers rose before God as a remembrance. Had Cornelius not prayed in *chronos* times, he would not have seen the *kairos* event, a series of divine encounters that led to the outpouring of the Spirit on the Gentiles!

Patience in the midst of intercession is never easy. Yes, I have seen the Lord answer many specific prayers in remarkable ways, but over my lifetime, I have been in very few extraordinary prayer meetings. Most of my prayer has been patient endurance. Just as water dripping on the same spot over years can wear away the hardest rock, so persistent prayer for the same request will produce a breakthrough. In truth, an accumulation of prayer releases awesome results, including judgments against demonic principalities and the enemies of God.

An Intercessor Highly Esteemed By God

A young man named Daniel learned this many centuries ago. As a teenager, Daniel was exiled to Babylon from his home in Judah. A member of the nobility, he was chosen to serve in the palace of King Nebuchadnezzar and to be taught in the "Babylonian University." Despite his exile, Daniel made up his mind not to defile himself. So he refused the king's food and wine and instead ate vegetables and drank water. This so pleased the Lord that He gave Daniel "knowledge and understanding of all kinds of literature and learning. And Daniel could understand visions and dreams of all kinds" (Dan. 1:17) so that none surpassed him in wisdom and understanding.[1]

Throughout these years in the palace of King Nebuchadnezzar, Daniel developed a pattern that served him well. "Three times a day he got down on his knees and prayed..." (Dan. 6:10b). For 70 years, possibly, he knelt at his window that faced Jerusalem and prayed, "Lord, take us home to rebuild the temple."

Imagine praying the same prayer for 70 years—not once a day, but three times a day. That's ordinary, persistent, *chronos* prayer. I'm sure that there were days when Daniel wondered if his prayers would ever be answered, but Daniel learned a secret that all intercessors must discover if they would be effective in their prayers. Daniel searched the Scriptures to understand the counsels of God. He was not praying mindless or wishful prayers, but ardent, informed petitions: "...I, Daniel, understood from the Scriptures...that the desolation of Jerusalem would last seventy years" (Dan. 9:2). He did so from a position of intimacy with God—as His friend: "You are My friends if you do what I command. I no longer call you servants, because a servant does not know his master's business. Instead, I have called you friends, for everything that I learned from My Father I have made known to you" (Jn. 15:14-15).

The Responsibility and Authority of Intercessors

To be God's friend is to receive the responsibility of prayer. This was Abraham's experience. When God was about to destroy Sodom and Gomorrah, He shared His secret with Abraham: "Shall I hide from Abraham what I am about to do?" (Gen. 18:17) God then laid on his shoulders the very fate of these cities.

What an awesome responsibility! Derek Prince says, "God has vested in us—His believing people on earth—authority by which we may determine the destinies of nations and governments. He expects us to use our authority both for His glory and for our own good. If we fail to do so, we are answerable for the consequences. Such is the message of Scripture...."[2] Daniel was faithful in this responsibility. For 70 years he dominated the political scene in Babylon, unflinchingly holding to the worship of Jehovah. Then, when he was old, the time came for him to change the very course of history. As was his custom, Daniel was coursing over the prophetic Scriptures. Suddenly his eye fell on Jeremiah 29:10—"This is what the Lord says: 'When seventy years are completed for Babylon, I will come to you and fulfill My gracious promise to bring you back to this place' "—and a flash of light exploded in the old prophet's heart. Daniel quickly checked his calendar. "It's time! It's time!" he cried. "Seventy years are up and we're going back to Jerusalem."

Now remember, Daniel's environment hadn't changed. What had changed was his understanding of God's plans and purposes. God had brought His prophetic friend into the divine know, into God's intelligence system. So Daniel humbled himself, confessed the sin of his people, and prayed for the fulfillment of the secrets God had revealed to him.[3]

Daniel's prayers were no mere routine. He knew the value of what he was doing. At another time, he had fasted and prayed for three weeks to understand a vision the Lord had shown him.[4] Prayer burst from his heart and found its way to the very Source of the universe. Why? Daniel exerted in the heavenly realm the authority of a holy life. For 70 years he had remained faithful to the God of his youth. Though he lived in Babylon, he had not allowed the spirit of Babylon to live in him. Therefore, his prayers were effective in binding the principalities and powers over Babylon.

Daniel's prayer from a pure, righteous heart so affected Heaven that the angel Gabriel came to him, saying, "As soon as you began to pray, an answer was given, which I have come to tell you, for you are highly esteemed. Therefore, consider the message and understand the vision" (Dan. 9:23). The first thing God said through His messenger was Heaven's estimate of prophetic intercessors. They are *highly* esteemed. Then the angel revealed what must yet happen to God's people.

Our world needs Daniels, intercessors who will study the Scriptures and live holy lives that give authority to their intercession. (An intercessor cannot bind demons when he or she is bound by them!) These men and women stand in the very counsel of God crying out, "What's on Your heart, God? Reveal Yourself to us. Speak, Lord, for Your servant is listening."[5] They want to know the timing and purposes of God and are willing to humble themselves—fasting, praying, and confessing individual and corporate sin—until they receive what they seek.

These highly esteemed of the Lord scare the devil. He's not afraid of experts in endtimes prophecy. They have little power. Rather he fears the men and women who understand God's plans for the *present* and are available for His use for birthing these prophetic purposes now. They give themselves to prayer and fasting, and carry authority in the heavens because of their holy, righteous lives.

Concerning this salvation, the prophets...searched intently and with the greatest care, trying to find out the time and circumstances to which the Spirit of Christ in them was pointing when He predicted the sufferings of Christ and the glories that would follow (1 Peter 1:10-11).

These are the people who bring about the *kairos* moments of God, the reopening of revival wells long closed. They labor for the coming salvation of God until it is revealed. They are the Annas and Simeons who continually stay in the Lord's presence, serving Him day and night with fastings and prayers, believing with faith that they will yet receive what God has promised—even if the promise was given many years before.[6]

Frank Bartleman, with whom my heart is so knit beyond time, was such a person. The Lord had given him a vision for Pasadena that he embraced with his whole heart. So captivated was he by this divine assignment, that he travailed in this way:

"We prayed for a spirit of revival for Pasadena until the burden became well nigh unbearable. I cried out like a woman in birth-pangs. The Spirit was interceding through us... By this time the spirit of intercession had so possessed me that I prayed almost day and night. I fasted much also, until my wife almost despaired of my life at times. The sorrows of my Lord had gripped me. I was in Gethsemane with Him. The 'travail of His soul' had fallen in a measure on me. At times I feared that I might not live to realize the answer to my prayers and tears for revival...

"On one occasion, Brother Boehmer [Bartleman's prayer partner] had an impression I was coming. He went to the little Peniel Mission and found me there. We spent several hours in prayer.... We often spent whole nights together in prayer during those days. It seemed a great privilege to spend a whole night with the Lord."[7]

This is the destiny of all true intercessors. God shares His secrets with us and enlists our aid to bring to pass all that He has already set into motion: "Surely the Sovereign Lord does nothing without revealing His plan to His servants the prophets" (Amos 3:7). He reveals His promises and prophecies to provoke us to pray with increased earnestness, purpose, and understanding. Then when the timing is right, He sends the travail to release His purposes. This is the key of the intercessor, the authority given by the Father: "I will place on his shoulder the key to the house of David; what he opens no one can shut, and what he shuts no one can open" (Is. 22:22).

It is no wonder that satan is threatened by these commited well diggers. They know the secrets of God and have been given the authority to bring them to pass. They spell doom for the reign of fear and wickedness that satan and his minions have perpetuated throughout history. Should we be surprised, therefore, that he tries to sidetrack them by convincing them that the prophecies and promises of God are an excuse to cease praying? Or that because a promise is long in coming, or is difficult, it is not worth the effort to pursue it?

We must not let this happen. Whenever God reveals His secrets to His people, it is always for the purpose of calling them to arise and birth through prayer and fasting all that He has shown them. To do anything less is to forfeit our authority in the heavenlies and to become passive spectators on the sidelines of history. God-given revelation always demands involvement.[8]

This involvement carries a cost. After Daniel stepped into the Lord's counsel he found himself in a lion's den.[9] We can expect no less today. A lion's den surely awaits all who refuse to compromise the burden the Lord has laid on their hearts. Nevertheless, we must persist despite the distractions, misfortunes, and bodily discomforts we experience. Like Daniel, we must be focused, undistracted, and determined, refusing to take no for an answer. This is true prevailing prayer.

Birthing the Purposes of God

God is calling forth intercessors to birth His purposes. Mario Murillo describes this all-consuming prayer:

"In revival prayer, a person presents himself before God to give birth to an act of God in his city. He is not muttering requests, he is suspending his very being between God and man. At first it is just words and petitions, but soon it envelops the person. He is reduced to one long, all-consuming declaration. His whole body becomes the prayer.

"Hannah achieved this state when Eli thought she was drunk....

"When he prayed for rain, Elijah literally assumed the position the Jewish women assumed in order to give birth. 'So Ahab went off to eat and drink, but Elijah climbed to the top of Carmel, bent down to the ground and put his face between his knees.' " (I Kings 18:42)[10]

Elijah had the prophetic word of the Lord that it was going to rain. In fact, we are told that he was granted power just to speak and command the rainfall: "As the Lord, the God of Israel, lives, whom I serve, there will be neither dew nor rain in the next few years except at my word" (1 Kings 17:1b). Yet Elijah still needed to birth the rain in prayer.

The sign of the Church is the woman in travail, according to Revelation 12.

A great and wondrous sign appeared in heaven: a woman clothed with the sun... She was pregnant and cried out in pain as she was about to give birth. ... She gave birth to a son, a male child, who will rule all the nations with an iron scepter. And her child was snatched up to God and to His throne (Revelation 12:1-2,5).

Whenever we see this travail, we can be assured that great spiritual events are just ahead! Something is being birthed in the realm of the Spirit. The Church in every generation, from Eve to Mary to the Bride of Christ, is in travail "for the sons of God to be revealed" (Rom. 8:19).[11]

In the weeks prior to John Arnott's coming to Mott Auditorium in December 1994, I had been meditating on the woman in travail as being the sign of the Church and had asked God, "Show me the sign." I will never forget the night He did just that. It was so amazing. During the ministry time at our fledgling Harvest Rock Church, many people were being filled with the Holy Spirit. Suddenly three women were seized with groaning and manifestations just like those I had seen in my wife when she gave birth to our children. I could hardly bear to look. Then the voice spoke, "This is the sign you asked for!"

Those women were birthing the revival in Pasadena and Los Angeles! Their pain and crying out were evidence of the secrets God had laid on their hearts and the work they were doing to bring His purposes to pass. They were literally experiencing the birth pangs of the revival that hit Mott Auditorium January 1, 1995. They were sharing God's birth pangs.

Many others are being overtaken by these birth pangs. Mario Murrillo graphically describes a travail he experienced over Berkeley, California, while he was trying to plant a work on the campus there:

> "It was 3 A.M. and for no earthly reason I woke up scream-ing. I sat straight up in bed and could not stop the mysteri-ous gusher of grief that was exploding from my soul.

> "I threw on my clothes and raced out of my house. I walked for miles, sobbing...

> "So there I was, staggering through the night desperately trying to find a place to release this torrent of prayer. Hours passed and I found a lake and buried myself in the thickest part of the trees and bushes.

> "To try to describe the travailing and unutterable groanings is futile. Simply believe me when I say that time stopped, my soul went behind the veil. All my life I had wanted to pray like that. I knew that heaven heard and that hell dreaded the answer that was to come.

"The very place of prayer seemed to shine with God's glory. Then, as I never had heard His voice before, Jesus said to me, 'The power of Satan in this city has been pierced tonight. Now you will see a breakthrough. I have given you this city.' ...

"[The next morning]...I felt elated that God had given me this city. I knew the frustrations of the past were gone. I zealously approached student after student, simply waiting to tell them that Jesus loved them.

"Then my hope was shattered. A tall, muscular, student radical flew into a rage. 'Jesus loves me, does He? Well, I hate Him and I hate you!' he said to me. And with that, he spat in my face and tore up my literature. A crowd was gathering to watch the preacher pay for being on campus.

"Standing there alone, I felt betrayed and totally humiliated. This was a despair I felt sure I would not recover from. Then, without warning, a pleasant-looking young man stepped right up to the radical and confronted him gently, but firmly.

" 'Do you know who this man is?' he asked. The radical, somehow knowing he should back off, calmed down and responded, 'No, I don't know who he is.' 'This is Mario Murillo, a man of God,' the young man said. 'And God has given him this city.' After saying that, he cast deep, confident, knowing, loving eyes on me. Those eyes looked deep within my soul and confirmed the promise God had made to me the night before. Normally, the kind of words he used would evoke laughter from the listening students. For some reason there was a sense of respect and recognition. The radical apologized for his behavior and I told him I accepted his apology. Then I turned to find the young man but he had vanished. An angel? I have wondered for years and I still don't know. What I do know is that on that day an awakening began and within two years we had prayed with almost 2,000 young people to be born again."[12]

This travail is God's means for bringing forth all that He has promised and purposed. Just as a woman cannot choose the moment at which she will give birth to the child she carries, so there is a birthing in the Spirit that comes spontaneously. It cannot be summoned up by mental exertion or induced by emotionalism! It comes by the Lord's appointment and in His timing. " 'Do I bring to the moment of birth and not give delivery?' says the Lord. 'Do I close up the womb when I bring to delivery?' says your God" (Is. 66:9).

Crystal Brown, an intercessor in our church, had a profound dream in which she watched a man walking along, interceding for his neighborhood. Suddenly he was overcome with travail. As he began to weep, his legs melted into the very ground that he was interceding over. The Lord then spoke in the dream saying, "This kind of intercession is by appointment only."

God is giving many such appointments in our day. If we want to see extraordinary revival, it will be birthed by extraordinary prayer.

During labor, a woman is totally focused on the task of bringing her baby into the world. In the months prior to delivery, she is able to continue with her normal activities, but when she goes into labor, the things that normally concern her become unimportant. All her strength, all her concentration, is on the task at hand. She wants nothing to distract her.

This is a type of the holy travail that God is sending on His faithful ones who have persisted in the *chronos* times and are now privileged to give birth in these *kairos* times. In this holy season, our focus is completely on our burden of prayer. There is a complete consecration to prayer that moves us beyond the routine of our daily lives into extended periods of prayer and fasting. The hunger for revival consumes us and all other things seem trivial, as they indeed are, in the light of the eternal souls of men and women that hang in the balance. Tears are our daily meat. Just as a woman cries out in labor, there is a weeping that consumes us.

As Paul Cain so urgently entreats us,

"We must have tears if we are going to see revival. If we have no tears it's because our hearts are parched. The gift of tears is more than a result of suffering that comes from living in a fallen world; it flows from feeling the pain and the suffering that the Lord Jesus feels for us. He is our High Priest, touched by the feeling of our infirmities. The shedding of tears shows that the heart is engaged. Where are tears today? ... Prayer and intercession is the most important work of the Church. Ministry in the last days is worth everything. It will cost everything. ... Ask God for the gift of tears and expect it. I tell you, there will be no public reaping without some public weeping. The greatest reapers in this world are the greatest weepers."[13]

Jesus Himself was not exempt from weeping as He fulfilled God's purposes for His days on earth. He clearly portrays this work for us: "During the days of Jesus' life on earth, He offered up prayers and petitions with loud cries and tears to the one who could save Him from death, and He was heard because of His reverent submission" (Heb. 5:7). All who follow in Jesus' footsteps, giving themselves to this ministry of tears, receive this sure promise: "Those who sow in tears will reap with songs of joy. He who goes out weeping, carrying seed to sow, will return with songs of joy, carrying sheaves with him" (Ps. 126:5-6). This is one of the few Scriptures where we are guaranteed a harvest! Those who sow with tears *will reap* the harvest.

I'm hungry for that harvest. When Rick Joyner gave the prophetic word that we can delay judgment in Los Angeles by redigging the wells of revival here in L.A., a flash of light exploded in my soul like the flash that must have gone off in Daniel when he realized that it was time to go home to Jerusalem. I have been praying for the redigging of the wells in Los Angeles for 14 years. *But now is the time!* By the grace of God we are setting our faces to seasons of prayer and fasting to birth that very purpose. We are determined. We will not stop until we see the harvest we seek.

But this *kairos* moment is not just for Los Angeles. Cities across America stand on the brink of disaster. Nations around the world are controlled by demonic principalities and the enemies of God. We need intercessors who by their very travail will pull down these principalities and close the mouths of these lions. We need spiritual warriors who will not be discouraged or distracted by the worst that satan can throw at them, but will consecrate themselves to digging the wells of revival where they live.

May there be such an outpouring of prayer and fasting in the Church that God comes to pull down the demonic strongholds that control our cities. May we, like Daniel, recognize the prophetic hour we are in and travail as long as is necessary to free our nations from the bondage of satan. Let us ask the Lord of the harvest to give our indifferent hearts the tears we need—tears of repentance, compassion, and grace. God is waiting and listening for your cry:

> "Heaven itself falls silent. The heavenly hosts and celestial spheres suspend their ceaseless singing so that the prayers of the saints on earth can be heard. The seven angels of destiny cannot blow the signal of the next times to be until an eighth angel gathers these prayers...and mingles them with incense upon the altar. Silently they rise to the nostrils of God.
>
> "Human beings have intervened in the heavenly liturgy. The uninterrupted flow of consequences is dammed for a moment. New alternatives become feasible. The unexpected becomes suddenly possible, because God's people on earth have invoked heaven, the home of possibles, and have been heard. What happens next, happens because people prayed. The message is clear: History belongs to the intercessors."[14]

Chapter 11

Atomic Power Through Prayer and Fasting

In 1987 several members of our church went on long fasts for 15 to 20 days, some 30 days. Nightly, our little band of fervent souls prayed with strong desire for the release of God's presence in our worship. The final Sunday of the fast a prophetic song came forth. As the spontaneous words—"we gaze into an open Heaven"—were sung, it was as if a bomb exploded above us and the heavens opened. Pandemonium broke out. People began running, dancing, crying, and shouting. One person began calling out, "I see angels!" Prophecy erupted among us. No one could preach. God had come!

The next season of our church life was one of high level atmospheric intensity. People were saved and healed during worship. New songs came forth. "First love" rested on the congregation.

What caused this greater glory—however humble and localized? Fasting with prayer. Prayer is powerful; but fasting with prayer is even more powerful. It can change not just your local meeting, but the world. In the words of evangelist Mario Murillo, "[We] stand before the greatest door in history. Beyond this door lie the most precious gifts of God. Beyond this door [we] will find the keys to the secrets of the heroes of faith who have gone before [us]. They shook their generations and they stood at one time where [we] now stand."[1] This door is fasting and prayer.

Isaiah 58 describes the fast that is acceptable to the Lord—one from a pure heart and right motivation. In that same chapter, he gives the incredible promises that attend such a fast. They are powerful rewards that change the course of human events:

> *You will be like a well-watered garden, like a spring whose waters never fail. Your people will rebuild the ancient ruins and will raise up the age-old foundations; you will be called Repairer of Broken Walls, Restorer of Streets with Dwellings* (Isaiah 58:11b-12).

Simply put, fasting and prayer open the wells for the continual watering of our cities with blessing and for the calling forth and restoration of our inheritance!

One such instance especially bears repeating. It was a well released in 1946 by Franklin Hall's book, *Atomic Power With God Through Fasting and Prayer*. That single spark enflamed thousands across America to go on extended fasts and to seek God for revival and the return of the gifts of the Spirit.

Hall himself records that by early 1947, he had spoken to 50,000 on the subject of fasting and prayer. One million pieces of literature had been distributed. History shows that multitudes of Christians joined in the call to fast like never before—not for just a few meals, but for 10 days, 2 weeks, 3 weeks, 40 days. The purpose, Hall stated, was simply "to bring about old-time revival of sinners converted, the sick healed, miracles worked, and the power of God demonstrated as He wills."[2]

The result? A great well opened up from which we still drink today! In the years that followed, a great healing revival broke out with men like William Branham, Oral Roberts, and T.L. Osborne being used of God to perform extraordinary miracles. Revival tremors shook the earth as the Latter Rain movement poured into our country from Canada. Bill Bright arose and began to spread his vision of college campus reawakenings. Billy Graham's ministry was released, and the Asbury College revival commenced. What a clear statement for the atomic power of prayer and fasting!

Gordon Lindsey, founder of Christ for the Nations and spokesman and catalyst for the healing movement of the 1940's and 50's, testified that fasting prayer was the master key to the impossible.[3] Scores of the most powerful ministers of that day regularly participated. In fact, the Latter Rain brethren wrote, "The truth of fasting was one great contributing factor to the revival… Previously we had not understood the possibility of long fasts. The revival would never have been possible without the restoration of this great truth through our good brother Hall."[4]

Now, 50 years after the publication of Hall's book, a Jubilee call to fasting is again being trumpeted in Bill Bright's book, *The Coming Revival*. In January 1996, after reading this book, I went on a 40-day fast of juices and water. Many of the people at our church in Pasadena, California, entered long fasts during that season. Out of our prayer and fasting was birthed a 24-hour, mostly continuous prayer meeting, now in its third year. In fact, the renewal meetings in our city were birthed in a 21-day city-wide fast called by Wesley Campbell. I believe this is a key that our generation must turn. It is God's gift for the Church.

This spring, I was blown away to see a front-page article in the *New York Times*, entitled "A Call to Fast, in Hopes of a Spiritual Revival." A headline like this in a world newspaper like the *New York Times* is a sure sign that something big is going to happen! The article contained the proof!

"Thousands of evangelical Christians, hopeful that the nation is on the threshold of a huge spiritual revival, have quietly taken to preparing by fasting and praying, on their own and in large groups. Now prominent evangelicals, led by Bill Bright of Campus Crusade for Christ and Pat Robertson of the Christian Broadcasting Network, are calling for 2 million Christians to join in a national 40-day fast beginning on March 1 and ending on April 9, [1998] the day before Good Friday.

" 'Fasting and prayer is the atomic bomb, or the hydrogen bomb, of all the Christian disciplines,' Bright said in a recent interview. 'Prayer has great power, but fasting with prayer has infinitely more power…'

"An unprecedented number of Christian leaders must believe it to be true. Last November, 800 church leaders from more than 60 denominations gathered in Dallas for collective fasting, preaching, and prayer. Their sessions were broadcast by satellite to about 2,200 churches, living rooms and campuses and were heard on more than 110 Christian radio stations."[5]

And there have been similar events across the land.

Fasting: The Secret Weapon of the Church

History reveals that prayer and fasting have always pre-ceeded great interventions of God in the affairs of man. They are consistently the precursors to flashpoints of Pentecost. Consider:

- Jesus fasted in the wilderness for 40 days and 40 nights before He was baptized and the Holy Spirit descended upon Him.[6]

- The early disciples were continually devoting them-selves to prayer in the upper room until the Holy Spirit fell on Pentecost.[7]

- The members of the early Church were fasting when the Holy Spirit told them to set apart Paul and Barnabas as apostles;[8] then the Church sent them out after prayer.

Likewise, revival history records the influence of fasting. One example is Azusa Street.

- William Seymour and his revival core fasted ten days before the outpouring of the Spirit on April 14, 1906, at Bonnie Brae Street. "Yes, the second Pentecost on

AZUSA in 1906 came about just like the first Pentecost. This latter rain outpouring of the Holy Spirit started with A TEN DAY FAST AND PRAYER SEASON in much the same manner as it did upon the 120 that 'continued with one accord in prayer and supplication.' "9

- One worker of the Azusa day stated: "The first thing that was done, before the power ever fell on Azusa, was a united ten day season of fasting and prayer. If there was ever any sectarianism, fasting broke it down." Another, who roomed next to Seymour, stated that Seymour "fasted for weeks at a time and only ate occasionally. There was much fasting and prayer in those days, and I believe another Azusa could be here today if God's people would get to travailing in much prayer and fasting."10

Today we face perhaps an even greater urgency and injunction to fast than ever before. Out of God's kindness, He is stirring the waters of renewal and revival across our land and the nations. But along with His kindness, we still face the severity of God.11

" 'As a nation, we are faced with the gravest crisis in our more than 200-year history, because we have rejected God and His Commandments,' warned Bill Bright while speaking last year… 'Judgement has already begun with rapid social disintegration during the last three decades, but far worse awaits us…unless believers truly repent, further judgement and ultimate destruction loom drastically ahead.' "12

Will we turn the key of fasting and prayer to change history? Joel 2 foreshadows our options.

The people of Joel's generation were facing similar days to those in which we live. It was a time of great national distress. While we often quote God's promises in Joel 2—"…I will pour out My Spirit on all people. Your sons and daughters will prophesy, your old men will dream dreams, your young men will see visions. Even on My servants, both men and women, I will pour out My Spirit in those days" (Joel 2:28-29)—we may neglect the words that precede this promise—"*And afterward....*" *Afterward* refers to a corporate gathering for prayer and fasting!

> *Declare a holy fast; call a sacred assembly. Summon the elders and all who live in the land to the house of the Lord your God, and cry out to the Lord* (Joel 1:14).

> *"Even now," declares the Lord, "return to Me with all your heart, with fasting and weeping and mourning. Rend your heart and not your garments..."* (Joel 2:12-13).

God promises to pour our His Spirit *after His people unite in corporate mourning and fasting*. Only then does He pledge to restore the land and send His Spirit!

This was a crucial directive for Joel's generation. Derek Prince explains:

> "If we turn back to the beginning of Joel's prophecy, we are confronted with a scene of unrelieved and total desolation. Every part of the inheritance of God's people is affected. All is blighted; nothing is fruitful. There is no ray of hope, no human solution. What does God tell His people to do? The remedy which God prescribes is united fasting: 'Sanctify ye a fast'...(Joel 1:14).

> To *sanctify* here means *to set apart*. God's call to fasting must have absolute preeminence. Every other activity, religious or secular, must take second place."[13]

Likewise, in this hour, God's call to "sanctify a fast" comes with renewed urgency to the Church in America. While some have entered into fasting, the need is very great.

A holy fast is God's prescription for our covenant-breaking, morally decayed society. Yes, some revival wells have been opened and we have seen evidence of a new outpouring of God's Spirit, but it's a trickle compared to the rushing waters He has in store. These wells of God's Spirit were first dug by our forefathers and mothers through prayer and fasting. Now it's our turn to do the same, thereby releasing the gushers of blessing, healing, and salvation.

I am not content until I see history changed! That's why I have prayed and fasted for 14 years, repenting for the sins of my city and begging God to reopen the wells of Frank Bartleman, William Seymour, Aimee Semple McPherson, Henrietta Mears, Billy Graham, Bill Bright, and others. You are called to be a history changer, too! May God grant you a greater grace and desire to further answer the call! For the very future of your sons and daughters, your neighbors and your loved ones, may well depend on it!

Effective Fasting and Prayer

Perhaps you've never fasted or you've fasted for only a meal here and there. Let me share some thoughts with you from my experiences, and those of others, so that you may be helped and encouraged and may receive the most from your wonderful obedience.

1. *Fast and pray to humble yourself and to purify your worship.*

    Remember, the purpose of fasting is to align your heart with God's heart. We are not trying to get something from God, but are seeking to realign our hearts' affection with His. To do this, we must do "holy violence to"[14] the "pleasures that wage war" (Jas. 4:1 NAS) against the soul and open a way for the Holy Spirit's passion to dominate us. In fasting we can more readily say, "We love You, Lord, more than anything in the world." Lust of any kind perverts worship, but fasting enables us to cleanse the sanctuary of our hearts of every other rival. As was true in Daniel's fast, the dominant emphasis must be on humility and confession, not the object we seek.

2. *Take time to pray and to read the Word.*

This may seem obvious, but busyness and distractions abound. What is the use of opening yourself to more of God, of His revelation, and of insight in His Word if you don't avail yourself of them?

Remember, this is a time when you can hear and respond more clearly—and often more powerfully—and can enjoy the presence and glory of God in a special way. Don't miss out on it!

3. *Have a clear target for prayer focus.*

Without a vision (a clear, prophetic prayer goal), people perish.[15] During a fast, I often pray into four or five prayer goals, but I must make sure that they are clearly articulated. When I'm not deeply motivated by a clear goal, I usually fast until break-fast! Write down the vision so you can run with it.[16]

4. *Do the fast with someone else.*

Two are better than one. If one falls the other picks him up.[17] Perhaps you have a prayer partner. Ray Clarke and I are prayer partners. Early in 1998 we completed a 40-day season of prayer and fasting to redig the wells of revival in Los Angeles. As part of our time together, we read the account of Frank Bartleman praying with William Boehmer. By praying and fasting with a partner, you may be more motivated to pray and fast for your goal.

5. *If you fail, don't give in to condemnation.*

The "fast or not to fast" schizophrenia can be a major tool of the enemy. Even though you may fail several times, God always extends grace. The Lord will give you fresh motivation. I remember one fast where I gave up and snuck some yogurt and chips. The next day an inter-cessor came to me and said, "I saw you in a dream. You were supposed to be fasting, but you were eating yogurt and chips." That was pretty good motivation to start again—and to realize that what I was doing must be of some significance!

6. *Make your commitment and determine the length of your fast.*

People often report that fasting is easier the longer you go. Historically, the most signficant results have come through extended fasts at the Lord's leading.

- A total fast is without water. Don't go beyond three days.

- A water-only fast is very difficult, but very effective. Depending on your weight and metabolism, you may go 40 days on water.

- A juice fast allows you to enter into the spirit of fast-ing, but still gives energy. Most people can do a 40-day juice fast. For this fast, drink small amounts of low-acidic or non-acidic juices. This gives you the desired effect of fasting, but also gives your body strength and needed minerals. Apple, cranberry, and watermelon juices are excellent, as is vegetable broth. It is best to schedule your juice intake. To drink juice continually may hinder the spirit of fast-ing and self-control. A non-diluted juice fast is much easier and is still very beneficial. For many people it may help to drink protein power drinks. This is especially advisable if you have health and/or weight considerations.

- A Daniel fast of vegetables and water is good for those employed in manual labor or for those who carry a heavy workload (like moms).

- A milkshake fast isn't really a fast!

7. *Prepare physically.*

Limit your intake of food to fruit for two days before an extended fast. Fruit is a natural cleanser and is easy to digest. If you can, stop using coffee several days before you fast. Prepare yourself for mental discomforts such as impatience, crankiness, and anxiety. Expect physical discomforts. You may experience dizziness, headaches, and different pains. The headaches are not a sign to stop fasting. Your body is working to cleanse itself of impurities.

8. *Prepare for opposition.*

Satan tempted Jesus during His fast, and we must expect the same. You can bet that someone will bring donuts to the office on the day of your fast. It is amazing how this works! Your spouse may suddenly be inspired to cook your favorite meals for the rest of the family. *Press through.* You may also feel tension build in your home. Work through this with your spouse. My fasts are just as difficult for my wife as they are for me. She, too, must be well prepared before I begin to fast. Likewise, discouragement may seek to overtake you like a flood. Recognize the source of the discouragement and stand on the victory of Christ.

9. *Fast in secret.*

Don't boast about your fast, but don't be afraid to let people know before you go to their homes that you won't be eating.

10. *Break the fast gradually.*

On an extended fast of light juice or water, your digestive system shuts down completely. This can pose a great danger if you are not careful. So as not to harm your body, you must exercise strong self-control when you begin to break the fast. Begin with several days of diluted, non-acidic juice. Then take regular strength juice and vegetable broth for several days. After a week, you may begin to drink light non-milk soups and thicker juices like V-8, carrot juice, and green vegetable juices. Fruit and vegetables may follow. I broke too quickly after one of my early fasts and nearly needed hospitalization. Be careful!

11. *Feel free to rest much and to engage in light exercise.*

12. *Seek medical advice and oversight before and during the fast if you have medical problems or are older.*

13. *Expect to hear God's voice through dreams, visions, revelations, and the Word.*

    Daniel prepared himself to receive revelation through fasting.[18] Prepare yourself in a similar manner, focusing on your goal and making sure that you understand what God is wanting to do. Then fast expectantly. God has promised that He will reward you.[19] A few months ago while ministering in Malaysia, a brother was "caught up into the heavens" during a 40-day fast. After the fast, he took a team into the interior of Borneo, where he saw a dead woman raised and revival break out in the village![20]

14. *Don't be discouraged if you don't see immediate results. Many times breakthroughs come after a fast— sometimes long after.*

    Do not listen to the lies that nothing is happening. It is my conviction that God rewards every person who fasts in faith.

When Jesus was baptized by John, the heavens opened and the Dove descended upon Him. Immediately thereafter, that same Dove drove Him into the wilderness to fast for 40 days and to contend with the territorial strongman over the earth, satan himself. For 40 days, Jesus warred through prayer and fasting to reverse the curse of Adam and Eve and to overcome the devil and release atomic power into the earth. The results recorded in Luke show that history changed forever through the strength and victory the Lord gained by His obedience. Divine power was now His! "Jesus returned to Galilee in the *power* of the Spirit, and news about Him spread through the whole countryside" (Lk. 4:14).

On the other hand, the Israelites spent *40 years* in the wilderness complaining about food and yearning to go back to the leeks and garlic of Egypt. They preferred captivity to the discipline of the wilderness.

America is in the wilderness right now. Our choice is this: Do we prefer captivity under the territorial strongmen that hold sway over our cities, our neighborhoods, and our loved ones? Or will we pray and fast until the curse of evil is removed from our land and the wells of revival are redug? If we want *apostolic results* like the power Jesus exercised, we must return to *apostolic methods.* It's our choice—40 years or 40 days!

Chapter 12

Prevailing Influence Through 24-Hour Houses of Prayer

One of History's Greatest Prayer Meetings

One morning during a fast early in 1996, I awoke at 5:15 a.m. The number on my digital clock jumped out at me. I sensed that God was speaking to me concerning a biblical passage, but I didn't know which one. I left my home and went across the street to my 2,500-seat prayer closet. There I began to seek the Lord.

As I waited before the Lord that morning, I read about the 1727 outpouring of the Holy Spirit among the Moravians. This community of believers held what must surely be considered one of the greatest prayer meetings in history: a 24-hour prayer watch that continued, unbroken, for 100 years! Moravians greatly impacted the great revivalist John Wesley. Their fervor for the Lord also birthed the modern-day missions movement.

As I read the story of their 1727 call to prayer, the Spirit of God began to groan deeply in my spirit. I knew that something was coming forth from the heart of God. So I began to pray, "Release the Moravian lampstand. Release the Moravian lampstand."

Later that morning, after I had returned home, the numbers on the alarm clock when the Lord had awakened me came rushing back: 5:15. God was calling my attention to Matthew 5:15! "Neither do people light a lamp and put it under a bowl. Instead they put it on its stand, and it gives light to everyone in the house." He was saying, "It's time to take up the Moravian lampstand and bring it out for all to see." God wanted me to help facilitate that lampstand for my city.

In these final days, God is going to release 24-hour houses of worship and prayer. He's going to reestablish the day and night ministry of the tabernacle of David. This tabernacle was God's favorite home. It was a tent in which there was no veil to separate God from His people. There was nothing pretentious about it, nothing exclusive. It was available to all. Every Israelite had unhindered, intimate access to the Ark of the Covenant and to the glory of God's presence. Here worshipers attended the Lord in songs and prayers.

I recently heard revival evangelist Tommy Tenney speak on these keys of David's tabernacle. His message burned deeply within me, putting into words what has been in my heart for years. My secret longing and ambition has been to see day and night worship and prayer ascend to the heart of God.

David also had such an ambition. His longing was to see and do on earth what was already being done in Heaven: "Your kingdom come, Your will be done on earth as it is in heaven" (Mt. 6:10). Why? First because David knew that there is a tabernacle in Heaven where continuous praise and worship take place before the throne of God.

Therefore, they are before the throne of God and serve Him day and night in His temple; and He who sits on the throne will spread His tent over them. Never again will they hunger; never again will they thirst. The sun will not beat upon them, nor any scorching heat. For the Lamb at the center of the throne will be their shepherd; He will lead them to springs of living water. And God will wipe away every tear from their eyes (Revelation 7:15-17).

Second, David recognized that such a spiritual tent on earth would be blessed by God and would become a place of rest, healing, and refreshing for His people. Hence, David pitched a tent, brought the Ark of the Covenant into it, and presented offerings to the Lord there. Then he appointed priests to stand and minister before the Lord in continual shifts. For 30 years the tent of Heaven rested on the land. This was a time in Israel's history of unprecedented blessing. All the enemies of God were defeated and the people of Israel rested in peace and prosperity.

God has promised that He will restore this tent: "After this I will return and rebuild David's fallen tent. Its ruins I will rebuild, and I will restore it" (Acts 15:16). I yearn to see the fulfillment of this promise. My cry has long been that the songs and prayers that filled David's tabernacle day and night for approximately 30 years would again find a home on the earth, that the Lord would again find a place to fill with the glory of His presence all day long.

Releasing the Moravian Lampstand

Through the years my heart has been gripped when others have spoken of the coming of such a dwelling place of God. I remember when I was reading an article by Jim Goll in 1993. I had met this prophet of the Lord only once, but his prophetic message calling the Body of Christ to intercession had gripped my heart. In the article, Jim declared that God was going to release houses of 24-hour prayer and worship in 120 cities on the earth. As I read, a cry went up in my heart. I ran from my "Pasadena for Christ" offices into Mott Auditorium and began to weep. "Come and do it here, Lord," I prayed. "I long for it here. Release David's tabernacle in this place."

Just then the phone rang in my office. "Oh, don't bother me," my heart cried. "I'm having this wonderful time of prayer." But I ran up the steps to my office and answered the phone. On the phone was my covenant friend Chris Berglund. I shared with him what I had been doing: "I've just been weeping. I'm longing for Mott to be a dwelling place for the Lord. I've been reading Jim Goll's article on 24-hour houses of prayer and I'm crying out for it to come here."

Chris, amazed, replied, "Unbelievable. I've just been listening to Jim Goll speak at the Los Angeles YWAM (Youth With a Mission) base. Just this moment, he stopped abruptly in the middle of his message and prophesied, 'Lou Engle. Mott Auditorium. 24-hour house of prayer.'"

I knew that God had ordained something special to happen in Mott Auditorium. He had promised me that when He told me to move beside the empty, dusty building. Now God was confirming another fulfillment of His promise. He desired to release a 24-hour house of worship and intercession.

When a prophetic word comes, you don't immediately go out and start making it happen. The word shows what is in God's heart and sets things in motion, but God will bring it to pass in the proper timing. So for two years I kept this vision close to my heart.

Then came New Year's Day 1995, when the renewal broke out at Mott Auditorium. Three months later, renewal minister Wesley Campbell spoke at Mott and challenged us to start nightly renewal meetings. "If you don't," he said, "someone else will." He also challenged us to start a 21-day fast to see if God would sustain the impact of the conference with John Arnott.

I felt in my spirit that this counsel was good. In truth, it is a principle of well digging: Strike hard and keep striking until revival breaks out. Then continue striking to sustain the outpouring of God's Spirit. So we called a 21-day fast and started daily morning and noon prayer meetings. Between 60 and 70 people began to seek God intensely; deep repentance and intercession attended those daily gatherings. These prayer meetings birthed the protracted renewal gatherings at Mott Auditorium. (Protracted meetings are costly, but they are necessary in creating enough spiritual momentum to impact a city.)

For one full year the Lord sustained intense prayer meetings, but it seemed that we were always moving them from one room to another. Then the Lord dealt with me concerning building a prayer room—a room that would be used only for prayer and worship: "…for My house will be called a house of prayer for all nations" (Is. 56:7). He wanted more for the intercessory ministry than only crumbs of provision.

Shortly afterward we began building a prayer room called "The House of Prayer for All Nations." A full wall map of the world now hangs on the wall in this room, and music from a stereo helps to create an atmosphere for worship. A carpeted altar and pillows lend themselves to times of sustained prayer. Just prior to the building of this room, I read Bill Bright's book entitled *The Coming Revival.* I made a determination to fast 40 days in January of 1996, during which time the Lord led us to pray for the release of the Moravian lampstand, to once again see continuous prayer released.

Some months before, I had been given a book on the Moravian revival and the corresponding prayer movement. Unfortunately I had lent it to someone and could not remember whom. So I asked the Lord to confirm that this whole series of prophetic events was from Him by having the person return the book. Within three days, the person stood before me, book in hand, saying, "I just remembered that I had your Moravian book!"

Yes! I knew that I was on a prophetic roll. Thus the vision of a 24-hour house of prayer and worship became our constant prayer and gave a spiritual focus to the 40 days of our fast.

One night part way through the fast, I spent the night in the prayer room seeking the Lord. During the night I fell asleep and had a dream. In the dream, an intercessor came to me and urgently exhorted me, "Don't leave the mountain of the Lord for ten days!" I woke up and sensed that God was directing me to spend the final ten days of the 40-day fast in the prayer room. I was to stay there day and night, and my children were to sleep with me there. Thus I determined to stay in the prayer room 24 hours a day, leaving only to take showers.

During those ten days, I felt that I should call Jim Goll. Before I could make the call, Jim called me. I couldn't believe it. Without my knowledge, Ché Ahn, our senior pastor, had scheduled Jim to speak at our church during those very ten days. I was quite stunned by the timing and knew that God was up to a supernatural birthing.

Jim spoke at Harvest Rock Church during the first weekend of February 1996. Amazingly, he began to share about his intercessory excursion to the original Moravian compound in Herrnhut, East Germany. I was all ears! Before Jim and his team left for the trip, God had told them that they would meet a man named Christian Winter, who would give them the keys to the compound. God also impressed Ezekiel chapter 37, where God resurrected dead bones, upon the hearts of the team.

When Jim and the intercessors with him arrived at the Moravian compound, they met Christian Winter, who gave them the keys to the ancient cemetery where many of the original Moravian pioneers had been buried. As they walked through the cemetery, Jim sat on an old tombstone. Looking at the head stone, he was astonished to see that he was sitting on the stone over the grave of Christian David, the founder of the Moravian movement. As Jim sat there, the Lord quickened Ezekiel 37:3— "Son of man, can these bones live?"—into his spirit.

As I listened to Jim recounting the story, my whole being was lit on fire. "Yes!" my heart cried. "These bones can live again here! Oh God, restore the Moravian 24-hour house of prayer and worship here in Mott Auditorium. Make this a birthplace of the redigging of the Moravian well!"

Meanwhile, Jim continued the story of his trip to the Moravian compound, telling how the intercessory team had been given the key to the watchtower where there had been continuous prayer by the Moravians. As Jim and his band began to prophesy to the wind according to the mandate in Ezekiel 37:9—"Come from the four winds, O breath, and breathe into these slain, that they might live"—a mighty rushing wind suddenly began to swirl all around them. The wind had come out of nowhere. Jim knew that it was a sign of the mandate the Lord was giving him to release 24-hour houses of prayer throughout all the world.

Jim later told us that in the days immediately following the trip, God had not released him to share the whole message of that intercessory journey. In fact, he had remained in seclusion throughout the month of January, speaking the full vision for the first time at Harvest Rock Church.

How excited I became as Jim spoke. God was entrusting us with that which is very dear to His heart. He was bringing the ancient tools of intercession from the archives where they had lain dormant for centuries. Worship, 40-day fasts, 24-hour-a-day prayer…these are the tools God has assigned to us in preparation for the greatest harvest of souls in the history of the world.

God confirmed the giving of these tools the night that Jim shared this message with our church. The Spirit of God descended on us in an amazing way and an explosion of power moved through the congregation. Ché Ahn, watching his wife manifest under the power, kept saying to himself, "My wife is wild." Then, suddenly, Ché flew through the air six or seven feet as the power of God hit him. I saw it with my own eyes. It was the apostolic power confirming the word delivered by God's prophet, Jim Goll. God was attesting to his message. Then Ché began to weep profusely. (He later said, "The terror of God hit me!")

Mott Auditorium is but one 24-hour house of prayer and worship that the Lord is seeking to establish. David's tent fell after 30 years. Centuries later, God raised up the Moravian tent. The Moravian tent also fell—this time after a remarkable 100 years. Now God is once again raising up a new house of prayer, a house that will contend with every other house of prayer in the earth.

God further provoked me to intercession for this new house of prayer through a dream he gave my friend Chris Berglund. Chris called me during my 40-day fast and described this dream in which he saw a Buddhist house of prayer sitting on top of a Christian house of prayer, dominating the Christian house. Something of a holy anger went off inside me and I began to pray and preach concerning the new house of prayer and worship that is arising, "May God raise up a house of prayer that will contend with the Buddhist house of prayer, the Muslim house of prayer; every material, worldly place to which man pays homage; and every other house of prayer throughout all peoples on earth."

Shortly after my fast in January 1996, which also happened to be the time of the Muslim 30-day Ramadan fast, I went on a journey to a hidden people group city. There is not one church among the three million people of this group. At 4:30 in the morning I was awakened by distant eerie-sounding chants. It was the Muslim first call to prayer. Within minutes every mosque in every neighborhood joined the call. It was as if a million principalities were boasting their spiritual dominion over the city.

The Muslim house of prayer is strong. Muslims pray to Allah five times a day. During the Ramadan fast, millions of Muslims across the world do not drink or eat during the daylight hours. What kind of spiritual power is released into the atmosphere by this sacrifice? Remember, sacrifice releases power in the demonic realm even as it does in the godly realm. It's no wonder that the Church has not been able to see many converts among the Muslims. I think, "My God, look at the Muslim house of prayer! How can we contend against that when we can't get Christians to pray once or twice a day or to fast one meal a day?"

God is changing this. He's raising up a house of prayer to contend with every other house of prayer. We have begun to see this change during these last years of the 1990's. The Church is fasting and praying like never before, and God is blowing holes in the Muslims' veil. The good news is that thousands of Muslims are being converted through dreams and supernatural encounters.

Exodus chapter 17 tells the story of another battle that was decided through the lifting up of hands. Joshua was in the valley fighting the Amalekites. Moses stood on the top of a hill with the staff of God in his hands.

> As long as Moses held up his hands, the Israelites were winning, but whenever he lowered his hands, the Amalekites were winning. When Moses' hands grew tired, they took a stone and put it under him and he sat on it. Aaron and Hur held his hands up—one on one side, one on the other—so that his hands remained steady till sunset. So Joshua overcame the Amalekite army with the sword. Then the Lord said to Moses, "Write this on a scroll as something to be remembered and make sure that Joshua hears it...." Moses built an altar and called it The Lord is my Banner (Exodus 17:11-15).

This battle was not won by the swords wielded by human hands alone. Prayer assured the victory.

We would do well to understand that the battles we face today will be won the same way. Since January 1996, Harvest Rock Church has sought to sustain a 24-hour house of prayer. Shifts of 1, 2, and sometimes 30 intercessors take their stand to raise the staff of the Lord. Many times our hands have fallen, but our stand of faith remains! God will restore the 24-hour house of prayer. He will restore David's tent of continuous worship.

Our vision is to see this day and night prayer go citywide. Even now 30 churches have each committed to cover the city of

Pasadena in prayer throughout an entire day. We are limping, but the seed has been sown. Soon, with God's help, we will see citywide centers of worship and prayer established around the world. This was God's mandate to me in 1996, when He said to me, "Lou, wherever you can, raise a house of prayer that will contend with the other houses of prayer that seek to dominate a city."

God has purposed that the Moravian lampstand will live all over the earth. May He raise up intercessors to make this vision reality, intercessors with a heart to restore the fallen tabernacle of David and to reopen the well of the Moravians.

I am beseeching God that your heart will be part of such a restoration, and that you, too, will pray:

> *Oh God, when will the faith and vision of the Moravians shine throughout the earth? When will the fallen tabernacle of David be restored? We pray in unity with thousands across the world that 24-hour houses of prayer and worship will again arise in the earth. Grant us the grace to do on earth what is already being done in Heaven. Stir within us a passion to raise up houses of prayer that will contend with the prayer altars to other gods that are found in every city. You alone are worthy to receive our continuous praise and prayer. We lift Your staff of victory in our hands. Oh God, may the tabernacle of David be restored, may the wells of the Moravians be reopened, and may You release and bring in the greatest harvest in the history of the earth for Your glory! Amen.*

Chapter 13

Roots, Shoots, and Names

Every single vine in the vineyard had been burned. Only small sticks of charcoal stubble remained. One by one, as the morning sun rose, battered family members made their way back toward the house to give a report. Perhaps just one of them had been able to save a portion of the field...

As they huddled together, garments charred and faces blackened from battling flames, each drew the same conclusion from the dismal interchange. All was lost. They had failed to save their only heritage...and their very livelihood for generations.

The winds had quickly swept the fire into a fierce rage across the countless acres of the once beautiful, rolling hills. The battle was too big for the few. Then suddenly, a young man sprang to his feet and ran breathlessly across the rows of ruin to an old, secluded family memorial some distance away. There, encased by a shrine of concrete and untouched by the violent flames, remained one small, living grapevine...a tribute shoot to the father, who generations ago, had planted the vineyard.

From that one shoot, the vineyard would live again...

I knew it was only a movie, but the ending struck me like a punch in the stomach. Though all appeared lost, an entire heritage could be regained by just one living shoot. That is the same promise God gives to you and me, and to this generation. It has been His promise throughout time. It is the promise of Jesus Himself.

> *A shoot will come up from the stump of Jesse; from his roots a Branch will bear fruit. The Spirit of the Lord will rest on Him—the Spirit of wisdom and understanding, the Spirit of counsel and of power, the Spirit of knowledge and of the fear of the Lord* (Isaiah 11:1).

This prophetic Scripture foretells the lineage of the Messiah, a direct descendant of David. He is a shoot from that same plant: "*See, the Lion of the tribe of Judah, the Root of David…*" (Rev. 5:5b). It is a wonderful parable of hope. At the time Isaiah prophesied of the coming shoot of Jesus, David's glory days were long past, Israel was in exile, the temple had been raided and was a shadow of its previous splendor, and evil kings like Manasseh had disgraced the kingly lineage. Yet there was hope because the root remained: "He grew up before Him like a tender shoot, and like a root out of dry ground" (Is. 53:2a).

This means that while the glory of a movement, a heritage, or a revival may no longer stand like the mighty trees they once were, the root remains, and it can revive! The spiritual descendants of those who have shaped the course of history may yet reclaim their destiny. In fact, they must.

Although roots provide hope and stability, they do not bear fruit. We must not go to the extreme of being so in awe of our forefathers that we are content to marvel at things long past. Rather we must become branches ourselves to see fruit in our own day and strive to ensure that new fruit comes in the next generation.

Notice that Isaiah describes Jesus as both a *root* and a *shoot*. Each of us shares these callings. When we become sons and daughters of God through the gift of salvation in Jesus

Christ, we are adopted into His heritage and become rooted in God's eternal family. As we mature and become more firmly rooted and established in Him, we become the means through which new shoots become attached to the family roots. In other words, we become both roots and shoots so that our sons and daughters, be they natural or spiritual, may continue our spiritual lineage.

The Scriptures contain an awesome generational promise that confirms this truth: "Your wife will be like a fruitful vine within your house; your sons will be like olive shoots around your table. Thus is the man blessed who fears the Lord" (Ps. 128:3-4). The implication here is that the father is the root, and the sons are the fresh new shoots. What was a shoot in one generation becomes the root for the next. (The Bible most likely speaks of olive trees in these passages. Interestingly, an olive tree always sends out new shoots before it dies.)

As both natural and spiritual fathers and mothers in this age, we are called to nurture the tender green leaves or shoots that are in our midst. It is our responsibility to ensure that the olive shoots springing up around our tables will mature to themselves bear fruit. This is an obligation we cannot treat lightly. The Scriptures provide valuable guidance how we might fulfill this responsibility.

Name Your Children Prophetically

Names are important to God. He uses them to expose the identity and destiny of His people.

No longer will you be called Abram; your name will be Abraham, for I have made you a father of many nations (Genesis 17:5).

As for Sarai your wife...her name will be Sarah...so that she will be the mother of nations... (Genesis 17:15b-16).

By renaming Abraham and Sarah, God was calling those things that were not as though they were.[1]

God also gives names as terms of endearment:

...[Bathsheba] *gave birth to a son, and they named him Solomon. Now the Lord loved him...*[and] *sent word through Nathan the prophet to name him Jedidiah* (2 Samuel 12:24-25).

Jedidiah means "beloved of God."[2] What intimacy and vulnerability of heart the Lord expresses through renaming Solomon! The great and awesome God stoops down to lavish unabased affection on His son and daughter.

As parents and prophets, we must cry out to God seeking His secret wisdom in working out the names of our children. We must steer away from the temptation to give them a certain name simply because we like the name, although that is important. We must name them prophetically.

Our third child was eight months in the womb, and Therese and I were seeking the Lord as to his or her name. We concluded that we would name the child Josiah if Therese gave birth to a boy. We told no one of our decision. Soon after our discussion, a dear friend, Jim Riley, burst into the house and began to prophesy, "The Lord says that you will have a boy and his name shall be Josiah." "You've got to be kidding me!" I exclaimed. The next day another friend, Sandi Tullis, called my wife and shared that the Lord had impressed upon her that we would have a boy and asked if we had thought of the name Josiah. Wow! "What manner of child will this be?"[3] is the joyous question on our hearts concerning our son.

God is serious about names. Even as I write this I am moved to tears by a precious passage I had never seen. Jacob is blessing Joseph and his two sons, Ephraim and Manasseh.

*Then he blessed Joseph and said, "May the God before whom my fathers Abraham and Isaac walked, the God who has been my shepherd all my life to this day, the Angel who has delivered me from all harm—may He bless these boys. **May they be called by my name and the names of my fathers Abraham and Isaac**, and may they increase greatly upon the earth"* (Genesis 48:15-16).

The words, "May they be called by my name and the names of my fathers," just leaped into my spirit. My oldest son, Jesse, was named after his great, great, great-grandfather, Jesse Engle. Jesse was an evangelist. In the late 1800's he volunteered, as a 65-year-old man, to lead the first Brethren in Christ missions team ever sent to Africa. He planted a church in Rhodesia and died there two years later. To my son I declare, "You are Jesse, called by the name of my forefather Jesse Engle." When asked what he wants to do, my son Jesse replies, "I want to be a missionary."

Our sixth child was born on August 8, 1997. We named him Jacob after Jacob Engle, my grandfather five generations back. Jacob's family had set out in 1752 with 30 others families to seek a refuge, a new home, in America.

> "It was a sad group of sorrowing mothers that gathered about Anna Engle, in whose arms lay a helpless babe, only a few months old...
>
> "During the voyage every infant in the entire company died and was buried at sea, save one... Not only was 'Jockeli' the only infant that survived, but he was by far the youngest of the company. And when the circumstances under which he was born, and the almost miraculous preservation of both mother and child were remembered, it was little wonder these grieving mothers gathered about Anna Engle and her little one... One by one they extended the parting hand, and...expressed the firm belief that God had in store a great work for the child..."[4]

My forefather Jacob Engle was converted in the days of the first great awakening in America and founded the Brethren in Christ Church. I am the sixth in this generational line. Oh, what a heritage for my son Jacob!

It is not enough, however, to name our children prophetically. We are also called to be fathers and mothers worthy of emulation: living in a godly manner, teaching our children the Scriptures, and being good stewards of the generational heritage that is theirs as well as ours. Name your children prophetically, then give them a heritage worth passing on.

I thank God, whom I serve, as my forefathers did, with a clear conscience, as night and day I constantly remember you in my prayers. Recalling your tears, I long to see you, so that I may be filled with joy. I have been reminded of your sincere faith, which first lived in your grandmother Lois and in your mother Eunice and, I am persuaded, now lives in you also (2 Timothy 1:3-5).

(This passage is especially meaningful to me since my mother's name is Eunice!)

But as for you, continue in what you have learned and have become convinced of, because you know those from whom you learned it, and how from infancy you have known the holy Scriptures, which are able to make you wise for salvation through faith in Christ Jesus (2 Timothy 3:14).

Frame Your Children Prophetically

During a season of fasting, my son Jesse and I were spending special time together in a Christian bookstore when we were both struck by the beauty of a painting on the wall. Storm clouds mysteriously covered a panorama of jagged mountain peaks. Pristine waterfalls descended into a lake that mirrored the mountains that surrounded it, and a family of deer was drinking by the banks. Underneath the painting were the words, "As the deer pants for the waters, so my heart longs for You, oh Lord!"[5] For several minutes our hearts were opened to this "window of Heaven" through which the Lord chose to speak to us.

That night, my son had a dream about this picture, a prophetic dream that showed we share a mutual hunger for God in the spirit and that God has birthed this hunger in Jesse as a life call. Today that picture hangs in our living room as a prophetic reminder to Jesse of God's invitation to heavenly sight. Often I say to my boy, "Jesse, my son, this is your destiny: to hunger and thirst for righteousness."

Many parents are fearful of presumptuously framing or marking their children's destiny through prophecy. "What if I try to shape their lives in a pattern the Lord has not intended?" they ask. I agree that this can be a real danger, but if we don't prophesy over their lives, someone else will. The world and its prophets, from advertisers to perverted rock stars, are only too eager to conform our children into images of their making. Don't give them the chance. Carefully mark out your children's destiny under the guidance of the Lord, and don't shrink back from boldly proclaiming the heritage God is showing you.

One biblical way to frame your children prophetically is to bless them. This is not only our privilege as parents but also a mandate from the Lord. Isaac blessed Jacob and Esau,[6] and Jacob blessed each of his sons.[7] We must return to this patriarchal pattern of declaring our children's futures out loud. Many times at night my children call out, "Dad, please come and bless me!" It's a significant privilege we can enjoy!

As we seek the Lord for our children, the Dreamer Designer places *His* dreams and aspirations for *His* children in our hearts. We must learn to trust these impressions from God, be they dreams, prophetic names, or sudden flashes of insight for our children. Under the guidance of the Holy Spirit, we must also become students of their personalities, shaping and calling forth their unique traits, and stewards of the prophetic words that are given to them. All are part of our responsibility to consistently remind our children of their heritage and to prepare them to walk out all that God has destined for them. My mother certainly did this for me. She was always saying to me, "There is something special God has for you to do."

Claim Your Children in Prayer

I am convinced that God wants His people to pray larger prayers for their children than they would think to pray. "Now to Him who is able to do immeasurably more than all we ask or imagine" (Eph 3:20a)—this is the God to whom we pray. Given the prophetic promises I have received for my children, I am imagining great things. Even these prayers, however, are not large enough because God can do considerably more than I can imagine. Like Jabez of old,[8] our prayers should be, "*Enlarge the boundaries of my faith for my children.*" Day by day these little prayers ascend to Heaven, where God collects them until the bowls of Heaven overflow in a *kairos* moment. I would rather pray the grand visions God has given me for my children and slightly miss His intent, than hide the prophetic promises in the sand, fearing that God won't do what I ask.

The Scriptures command us to ask boldly: "Ask and it will be given to you; seek and you will find; knock and the door will be opened to you. For everyone who asks receives; he who seeks finds; and to him who knocks, the door will be opened" (Mt. 7:7-8). Men and women throughout the ages have done this, including people whose stories are told in the Bible. Consider, for example, Bathsheba's intercession before the aged and dying King David on behalf of her son Solomon: "And she said to him, 'My lord, you swore to your maidservant by the Lord your God, saying, "Surely your son Solomon shall be king after me and he shall sit on my throne" ' " (1 Kings 1:17 NAS). David's covenantal promise is the grounds for Bathsheba's request. She is baptized with covenant confidence and godly ambition as she intercedes for the promise to be fulfilled.

May this generation of moms and dads forge the future of their children on the anvil of daily, large, visionary prayers to the Father who declares, "'Call to Me and I will answer you and tell you great and unsearchable things you do not know [that will blow your mind]" (Jer. 33:3). May our attitude be like that of Bathsheba, refusing to be denied what God has promised. Then we will see a generation arise that will turn America back to the Lord. Our children will be "the hinge of history" that averts judgment and releases God's blessings.

I know for certain that prayers by godly parents do shape the lives of children. I will never forget the morning my mother stood, having arose early to have her morning devotions, and turned to me, saying, "Son, let me show you what I have been doing most every morning for years." She knelt on the floor before me and began praying for her children by name, calling forth God's blessings and purposes upon them. It was one of the most holy moments of my life. The scene is indelibly etched upon my memory and is certainly in God's "Book of Remembrances."

To this day my brother, my sisters, and I are the beneficiaries of our mother's prayers. Every one of us serves the Lord as men and women. My sister Connie is married to a church planter and leader in the Brethren in Christ denomination. My brother Vaughn is a schoolteacher who loves God and affects hundreds of kids through his godly life and witness. For 13 years he has helped to sustain a teachers' prayer meeting in his school. He also ministers to the poor and has a calling to full-time pastoral ministry. My sister Lucy is married to the pastor of the Calvary Chapel in Santa Maria, California, where 700 people pour into the church, seeking the Lord. Truly we are loved and blessed because of our father, Jacob, and are held by the prayers of our mother, Eunice.

No prayer is too small to shape the lives of our children. My wife, Therese, and I have seen this repeatedly in our family. At one point we had been praying for our oldest daughter, Christy Joy, that God would especially show her His personal love for her. As we vacationed back East with relatives, Christy was quite struck by her cousin's "prayer doll." She couldn't put her down, gleefully dragging her everywhere she went. She was especially thrilled by the velcro hands and feet on the doll, which allowed it to kneel in prayer. The doll's wide-eyed innocence actually reminded Therese and me of our precious daughter. Therese commented how great it would be if we could get a doll like that for Christy, but the trip was too soon over, and Christy Joy returned to Los Angeles empty-handed.

I had returned to L.A. earlier in the week. When I went to the airport to pick up my family, I carried a box for Christy Joy. An intercessor had been shopping at a thrift store when she found a very unusual doll, which she purchased and took home to fully clean and restore. She approached me at a prayer meeting that week, saying, "Lou, I have this doll that the Lord told me is for your daughter." Was Christy ever surprised! Her wide eyes and happy smiles were all Therese and I needed to assure us that God had indeed heard and answered our prayers. He had given her the very same kind of doll—some 3,000 miles from where she had left the other—and a permanent mark of joy in her heart to show His great love for her!

Never underestimate the power of your prayers for your children. They can be the catalysts that release God's many gifts and blessings.

Build Family Altars to the Lord

One memory of my father from my childhood stands out more than the rest. I will never forget the Sunday morning at the Upland Brethren in Christ church when I saw my dad, Gordon Engle, kneeling at the church altar at the end of the service. I was shocked by the depth of his emotion before God, by his weeping swollen eyes. It seemed to me that he stayed there forever. To this day I have not asked him what went on that day. It was too holy a moment. All I know is that the scene will be forever engraved in my mind.

Another memory of altar building comes to mind. It was in the days when I was leading the Pasadena for Christ prayer ministry; we were $1,000 behind our monthly budget. Gathering the family together, I shared the situation and asked my oldest son, Jesse, to pray. The day before our family prayer meeting, a man had been moved to write a $1,000 check for our family. He had never done anything like this before; nor has he since. But that month the Lord led him to meet our need. When I returned home that night, I gathered Therese and the children together and exclaimed, "Let me show you the glory of God." Laying the check before them and God, we built an altar, a memorial to the provision of God.

Another day I was moved to gather my family together and declare the mighty acts of God throughout the history of my family. As we held this covenant renewal service, I gave each of my children an unlit candle. I held the only lit candle, commemorating God's covenant with my forefathers: Jacob, Henry, Jesse, Jacob, Homer, and Gordon. I told my children about these men of God and how they had changed history with hearts on fire for God. Then I challenged them to be faithful to the covenants these men had made. "They are watching from Heaven," I told my children, "saying, 'Will Lou's children keep the flame alive that has been burning in our family for seven generations?' " Then I soberly exhorted them, "Kids, it's up to you. You must renew the covenant for your generation. You must choose to love the God of your forefathers." My children then took the candles they held and lit them as a symbol of their commitment to continue the heritage their forefathers had passed on to them.

Perhaps these stories bring memories to your mind of times when you, or some member of your family, built an altar, a memorial to the Lord. These are important memories, memories that need to be preserved because God saw these ceremonies and remembers the covenants He made with your forefathers and mothers. Now He looks to bless the next generations. Family altars unto the Lord are a significant way to root your children in their spiritual heritage.

Train Your Children Prophetically

In the last days...I will pour out My Spirit on all people. Your sons and daughters will prophesy, your young men will see visions, your old men will dream dreams. Even on My servants, both men and women, I will pour out My Spirit in those days, and they will prophesy (Acts 2:17-18).

We are seeing this prophetic explosion today. Men, women, boys, girls: all are receiving this gift of God's Spirit. God expects us to cultivate the prophetic gift in our children and to train them to use it. Here are some practical ways to cultivate this precious gift that Paul esteemed above all others.

First, help your children to develop a sensitivity for hearing the voice of the Lord. Almost daily I ask my children if God gave them dreams the night before. This simple question helps them to cultivate a hearing heart. Though I rarely have significant dreams and have never had a full-blown vision, my children do and are excited about God's involvement in their lives prophetically.

Second, be sensitive to the dreams God may give you concerning the destiny of your children, and teach them to be sensitive as well. Several years ago I read an article (now lost) in the *Los Angeles Times* about a woman named Christine Noble. Christine was quite young when her parents left her and her siblings. She was then shipped off to foster care, where she was repeatedly molested. As a young teen, she found herself on the streets, homeless, and was terribly raped. Somehow, despite the emotional wounds and scars, Christine pulled the broken pieces of her life together. Then one day the God of dreams, who has written an entire book on each of our lives,[9] unfolded a new chapter of Christine's book in a dream. She saw herself on the dusty streets of Vietnam with hundreds of disinherited, homeless, limbless children. These children were crying out, "Come and help us! Come and help us!" This was Daddy's dream for His broken daughter. Twenty years have passed since Christine saw herself in this dream. She has ministered to more than 60,000 disinherited Vietnamese children.

God has also been speaking to my son Josiah through dreams. He has received four dreams with the exact same occurrences. In the dream, Josiah walks with Jesus from His birth to His ascension. Along the way, he sees healings, Lazarus raised from the dead, and on and on. On the fourth occasion of this dream, my wife, Therese, suggested, "Let's do listening prayer, Josiah, and ask God why He keeps giving you this dream." We all closed our eyes and waited on the Lord.

Suddenly Jesse broke the silence excitedly, "I just had a vision of Josiah preaching in that big church in Colorado where Ted Haggard pastors." Then, to all our surprise, Josiah, with big beaming eyes, burst out, "I saw the same thing too!"

This experience and many others have forged and honed my prayers for my children. I pray the dreams! As one man said, "We shouldn't so much *stand* on the promises as *kneel* on the promises."

Third, be alert for dreams that establish or renew covenants. One early morning toward the end of 1997, I was wrestling inwardly in prayer with the fact that the revival power at Mott seemed to be diminishing. We had seen great Holy Spirit power for more than two years, but the power was no longer so strong. So I cried out to the Lord, "God, is there more revival coming to Mott Auditorium? If there is, give me a sign. Show me You are renewing with my children the covenants that are upon my life. Give one of my children a dream this morning as a sign."

I came home to find Jesse sitting on the couch with his open Bible. With tears filling his eyes, he said, "Dad, I just had this awesome dream! In the dream I was sleeping when someone suddenly shook me and urgently said, 'Get up! There is a great revival coming to Mott Auditorium.' " Oh, praise God! He keeps His covenants of love to a thousand generations. His judgments last for four generations, but His blessings are unto a thousand generations of those who love and obey Him.

God has many treasures to reveal to our children in dreams. We must learn the language of the Holy Spirit—the pictures close to our children's hearts that bring comfort, warning, correction, and encouragement—and we must take every opportunity to teach them to understand God's voice. My six-year-old son Jonathan had a vision. He was suddenly awakened to see a scroll roll out on the wall. On the scroll were written the words, "Harvest Rock Church—Pray for all nations."

The next morning he asked, "What's a vision?" I used that moment to teach my children about visions. Then I said, "Jonathan, the God of the whole universe stepped down to you last night and shared His heart for our church with you. God sure loves you to tell you the secrets of His heart like that."

How very true! God does love our children and He's nurturing the shoots that are growing from our roots! As parents we must be careful to take advantage of every open window moment both to recount the stories of what God has done in the past and to encourage our children's hearts that God loves them personally and has plans for their lives, too.

The following dream, given to my oldest son, Jesse, reveals that God is indeed inviting our children and youth to be actively involved in His service at an early age. It has been an intimate invitation for my children to enlist in "the wars of the Lord" now.

In the dream Jesse saw a good gang fighting a bad gang. One young man asked the leader of the good gang, "How old do I have to be to join?" The leader responded, "The rules have changed. It used to be 21, but now it's 12."

Jesus began His Father's business at the same age![10] There's a whole generation of "shoots" just waiting to be enlisted. As "roots," may we bless them to seek after Him now. May we encourage them to receive the dreams and covenants God wants to give them this very hour. May we release life to the next generation. Our fruitfulness in God depends on it...not to mention the future of our neighborhoods, cities, and nations!

Chapter 14

Elisha's Bones Still Live

The year was 1988. We had been in Pasadena for four years with no evidence of the harvest God had promised us. Filled with a deep sense of failure and experiencing a profound crisis of vision, I wept bitterly before my fellow elders during a staff meeting. They graciously released me to a two-month sabbatical.

During that time, I took an eight-day fast and visited the Pasadena Public Library. While reading the revival history of Pasadena, my heart was profoundly opened to my own destiny. In the stories I read I found, so to speak, my own name written there.

King Josiah also found his name written in the archives of history. A godly young man, Josiah could not look to his father for guidance and destiny. Indeed, his father and grandfather had been the most wicked kings in the history of the Southern Kingdom.

Amon was twenty-two years old when he became king.... He did evil in the eyes of the Lord, as his father Manasseh had done. ...he worshiped the idols his father had worshiped, and bowed down to them. He forsook the Lord, the God of his fathers, and did not walk in the way of the Lord (2 Kings 21:19-22).

Josiah was determined to leave a different legacy. He ruled Jerusalem for 31 years with a righteous heart, fulfilling the prophecy spoken of him, that he would destroy the altar at Bethel.[1]

And he did right in the sight of the Lord, and walked in the ways of his father David and did not turn aside to the right or to the left. For in the eighth year of his reign while he was still a youth, he began to seek the God of his father David; and in the twelfth year he began to purge Judah and Jerusalem of the high places, the Asherim, the carved images, and the molten images (2 Chronicles 34:2-3 NAS).

Now whose son was Josiah? Was his father Amon or David? His father was David! He belonged to a generational *line*, not just an immediate descendant. Josiah had to flip way back in the pages of his family scrapbook to find a mentor worthy of emulation. He chose David as the father after whom he would model his life.

John the Baptist also found the description of his own life in the annals of history. Can you imagine the fire of God that entered John when he read Isaiah 40:3—"A voice of one calling: 'In the desert prepare the way for the Lord; make straight in the wilderness a highway for our God' "—and the words were quickened to his spirit, "You are the voice! The time is now!"

Spiritual Grafting

Elisha died and was buried. Now Moabite raiders used to enter the country every spring. Once while some Israelites were burying a man, suddenly they saw a band of raiders; so they threw the man's body into Elisha's tomb. When the body touched Elisha's bones, the man came to life and stood up on his feet (2 Kings 13:20-21).

What an amazing passage of Scripture! The anointing of the Holy Spirit on Elisha lingered on in his bones like radiation, even after death! A man was raised to life simply by touching his bones.

That day in the Pasadena Public Library as I read the account of Frank Bartleman's life, I was given a new reason for living. Elisha's bones raised me from the dead!

I believe that the same thing happens spiritually when people come into contact with books or other records of revival history—particularly of their own ancestors. The dead are given new life as destiny replaces aimlessness and godly expectation supplants hopelessness.

This is good news for those of you who may say, "I don't have a generational blessing. My forefathers were not godly and my line is cursed." You may not know it, but an ancestor down your line may have prayed for you. You may be a partaker of a generational blessing that has been interrupted for a century. Maybe God has chosen you to be the "repairer of the breach," the restorer of the foundations of many generations! I don't know which is a higher calling, to sustain the generational blessing or to restore it.

God is your Father. If no historical accounts of your forefathers exist, or if your forefathers were unrighteous, there is an ancient story that describes the greatest Father of all. The Bible is that account. To know God as your Father is to have life filled with purpose and divine destiny. He is pleased to include you in His family and to give you other fathers in the faith.

Wow! This must be what the apostle Paul was talking about when he wrote to the Corinthians: "...for in Christ Jesus I became your father through the gospel. Therefore I urge you to imitate me" (1 Cor. 4:15-16). The Corinthians were being grafted onto another root through the ministry of Paul! They received a new heritage and inheritance. They could look to Paul and find a mentor worthy of emulation.

If your parents or family offer no godly lineage, you can be grafted into a holy line! You can find your inheritance elsewhere: "...you, though a wild olive shoot, have been grafted in among the others and now share in the nourishing sap from the olive root" (Rom. 11:17).[2] In fact, the best olive trees are not grown from seed, but from cuttings from cultivated trees. Perhaps this is your heritage or one that you will help bequeath to another.

Even if your family line is godly, you may still find your particular destiny by being grafted onto another root. This is what happened to me when I read the stories of Frank Bartleman. I knew without a doubt that I was called to redig the well of revival that he had dug in Pasadena.

Sometimes this grafting into the spiritual heritage of another person is evident in the events that surround a child's birth. These events then become the launching pad for great spiritual insight that we, as parents, are called to steward wisely.

On May 28, 1995, I received a phone call at 1:00 a.m. from two 11-year-old girls: Joy Ahn, Ché's daughter, and Christine Codiogan. "Come to Mott, come to Mott," they shouted. The two had been sleeping at Ché's home when the Holy Spirit came upon them powerfully. They woke Joy's mother, Sue Ahn, asking her to take them quickly to Mott Auditorium. They were being drawn by the glory of God.

When they stepped through the doors, their spiritual eyes were opened. Visions of angels and prophetic senses of revival burst out before them. They would cry aloud, "Mott's too small. Mott's too small. Stadiums will be filled!" I wept and recorded for three hours.

The girls ecstatically described angelic beings, each giving the same description at the same time. They also saw a ladder descending from Heaven to earth with angels going up and down. At one point they saw Vince Lombardi in Heaven. When I asked them if they knew who he was, they said that they had never heard of him, but that he had a football helmet on. I exploded with wonder. God has a super bowl coming to the Church!

This was a night of an open Heaven over Mott Auditorium. At 4:00 a.m., I walked across the street to my home. At 4:15 that morning, my wife, who was pregnant with our fifth child, started to go into labor. A few hours later a daughter was born to us. We named her Gloria (for the glory) Angela (for the angels) Grace (for God's favor) Engle (which is German for "angel").

Ché came to the hospital the morning of Gloria's birth. He didn't know if the child had been born yet, but he sensed that we would have a girl who would carry a blessing like Aimee Semple McPherson. When he shared this with us, my heart said, "Yes! Let it be done to her according to Your word."

Early in 1998 I was lying in bed with my two-year-old little "Glory." I began to talk with her about the morning of her birth. "Glory, you were born the night the angels appeared at Mott." Then I told her the story of that night's glory and the words Ché had prophetically spoken concerning Aimee Semple McPherson. "Aimee saw angels, worshiped God, and healed sick people," I told Glory. Then I looked into her eyes and said, "Glory, you may have the same gifts as Aimee." Glory looked at me without blinking her eyes. Then, with somberness and a profound sense of understanding, she replied from her heart, "Thank you." My heart leapt inside. Could it be?!

Parents, your children do not belong to you alone, but to your forefathers, and ultimately to our heavenly Father "from whom His whole family in Heaven and on earth derives its name" (Eph. 3:15). You must not shrink back from the spiritual destiny God gives to your children. Gather the prophetic promises spoken over them and claim them in prayer. Plant the seed of destiny often in believing hearts! You never know into what spiritual root God may choose to graft your child. You also don't know what child God may choose to graft into your root.

The prophet Zechariah saw two olive trees in a vision. These trees were dripping oil into bowls that sat atop a golden lampstand, supplying it with oil. If the oil is the Holy Spirit[3] and the lampstands represent local churches,[4] who are the olive trees? Frank Damazio suggests that they are the leaders in the local churches, and that one of the main functions of the apostles and prophets is to "drip" their anointing into the church as they exercise their gifts, particularly into the young olive trees of the next generation.[5] Ephesians chapter 4 would seem to support this understanding.

It was He who gave some to be apostles, some to be prophets, some to be evangelists, and some to be pastors and teachers, to prepare God's people for works of service, so that the body of Christ may be built up until we all reach unity in the faith and in the knowledge of the Son of God and become mature, attaining to the whole measure of the fullness of Christ (Ephesians 4:11-13).

The giving of gifts or anointing is for the building up of the Body of Christ so that *all* may mature into the fullness of Christ. One of the best ways to build up the Body is to shepherd the youth of the next generation into the same giftings. As spiritual fathers and mothers, we have a responsibility to the tender green shoots in our midst. It is all too easy for leadership to focus on administration or preaching and fail to nurture the next generation of leaders.

In the words of the apostle Paul, "Even though you have ten thousand guardians in Christ, you do not have many fathers, for in Christ Jesus I became your father through the gospel" (1 Cor. 4:15). As *The Message* explains, "There are a lot of people around who can't wait to tell you what you've done wrong, but there aren't many fathers willing to take the time and effort to help you grow up." We lack fathers and mothers who will ensure that the olive shoots springing up around our table will survive and mature to drip oil themselves. It is not enough for us to be branches; we must also be roots! This is the hope for our fatherless generation.

Elisha had a natural mother and father whom he loved. Yet he knew that his destiny did not lie with his father's oxen and plow, but with an old man in a cloak. Elijah also knew that Elisha's destiny was bound to him. When the still small voice of the Lord had spoken to him on Mount Horeb, he had received three assignments: to anoint Elisha as prophet, to anoint Jehu as king over Israel, and to anoint Hazael as king over Aram.[6]

Many know the story of Elisha pleading for Elijah's mantle near the Jordan River. Elisha did receive the double portion of Elijah's mantle, as he requested that day, but the giving of this mantle had truly been done years before when Elijah first threw it over the young man's shoulders. Elisha inherited Elijah's mantle not merely because he was present when the chariot of fire took the old prophet away, but because of the years of faithful mentoring he had received.

Passing on a spiritual mantle is one of the most important things a mature leader can do. This may occur with a single, powerful laying on of hands, but more frequently, a mantle is passed through a long-term investment of spending time together. Cultivating young olive shoots, be they from your natural lineage or not, is what making disciples is all about.

This task was supremely important to Jesus. Even more important than preaching to the crowds or healing the sick was the time He invested into His disciples. Making disciples is a time-consuming task. It requires relationship and commitment. It is not as glamorous as being a well-known speaker, and its impact may not be seen for years, but the importance of investing yourself in the next generation cannot be overestimated. In fact, you may not be able to complete your God-given purpose unless you pour yourself into the next generation. Elijah completed only the first of the three assignments God gave him on Mount Horeb. He anointed Elisha, his disciple, to be prophet after him. Elisha completed the other two.

There are some spiritual tasks that we may have been clearly assigned—even by the audible voice of God—whose fulfillment depends entirely on our anointing the generation to come! Elijah was raised up primarily to confront the ravages of the Baal worship introduced by Jezebel and to restore the hearts of Israel to the God of their forefathers. He is remembered for his fiery confrontation with Baal. What is often not understood, is that the most damaging attack Elijah made on the territorial spirit of Jezebel was done when he anointed Elisha! It was Elisha who completed Elijah's mission to anoint Jehu—who massacred the house of Ahab and removed the Baals from the high places—something even Elijah was unable to do in his day.

Had Elijah failed to invest in his spiritual son, who knows what the spiritual history of Israel might have looked like. The same can be said about Moses. Moses took Joshua up the mountain into the presence of God, he taught Joshua the Law, and in many other ways spent years preparing Joshua for his role as Moses' successor. Had Moses not invested in Joshua, his spiritual son, the Israelites may never have entered the Promised Land because it was Joshua who completed what Moses could not finish.

Joshua was rooted in Moses (just like Elisha was rooted in Elijah). Even the name by which he was frequently called—Joshua son of Nun—means "to resprout" or "to grow up from a root!"

As I travel around the nation speaking to youth, I am committed to giving them revival history. Often I have felt their hearts burn with hope. When I call the hungry forward and lay my hands on them, seeking to impart a mantle of revival hunger, many are changed by this impartation.

Perhaps you are young and reading this book. If you want to be fruitful, get rooted now! If your natural roots are unproductive or do not match the destiny you sense in your spirit, ask God to graft you into another spiritual inheritance. Seek the Lord for a spiritual parent if you have not yet found a mentor after whom you can pattern your life. If you do have a spiritual parent—be that your natural parent or a spiritual parent the Lord has given you—accept the discipline and teaching he or she gives you. Make it your commitment to study revival history and to dig the wells of revival that are your inheritance!

If you are older in the Lord, I simply need to ask you: Is the book of your history before the Lord able to raise anyone—including your descendants—from the dead when they read it? Are you building altars for the Lord in hearts that are on fire for Him? Will you be known more like Abraham, who continually built altars of sacrifice and worship for the Lord—or are you like Nahor—his little known brother who most likely spent his lifetime building a city in honor of himself?

It's not too late to rewrite your history! Search out and steward the promises made to your forefathers. Assume your responsibility to pass on their stories—both the good and the bad—to confess their sins, and to renew their covenants. Pass on your mantle, lest you fail in fulfilling your own call and commission. Disciple the sons and daughters God has given you in the ways of the Lord.

If we do not disciple our sons and daughters, the repercussions will be devastating. David failed to disciple his sons and his family's control over the Northern Kingdom ended with the death of Solomon. Eli failed to disciple or discipline his sons and his family lost the right to be priests before the Lord.

We must not fail in our responsibility. The stakes are too high. We must serve the next generation with our love and our prayers, whether they are our natural or spiritual children.

His Mysterious Ways

We are seldom aware of the impact of discipleship and prayer—but history may hang in the balance! I was stunned as I read the following account from an old *Guideposts* magazine.

"It meant a day out of our vacation, but my wife and I strongly felt that we should make the effort while we were in Maine to go see Dr. Reuben Larson, an 80-year-old missionary pioneer. After lunch during our visit, quite out of the blue, Dr. Larson asked, 'Ed, in all your travels have you ever run into an Indian named Bakht Singh?' How extraordinary! Only two weeks before, on one of his infrequent visits to the United States, Bakht Singh had invited me to lunch. I told Dr. Larson what I'd learned about Singh, how he was one of India's best-known Christian leaders, how he had founded hundreds of churches and had preached to thousands. Whenever he traveled, believers gathered at train stations to speak and pray with him for just a few minutes. The things I told about this godly man had a strange effect on Dr. Larson. He was literally openmouthed. Finally he explained why. 'Many years ago in western Canada I met a young Indian engineering student who was interested in the Christian faith. His name was Bakht Singh. For 50 years I've been praying for him, praying that he would come to know God better and serve Him. I've always wondered what became of him.' It wasn't long after our visit that Dr. Larson died. But even before then I knew why we'd taken that day out of our vacation to see him. We were meant to bring him the news that he had waited 50 years to hear."[7]

God's ways are so different from our own. He may be using you to prepare the next Joshua or Elisha. The training and prayers you give today may mold the next William Seymour, Billy Graham, or T.L. Osborne. The young man or woman you disciple this year may be the next John Wesley or Henrietta Mears.

What a challenge! We cannot afford to lose the next generation. The missionaries who will go to the unreached tribes on our planet are kneeling today in a high school prayer meeting. The martyrs who will gladly suffer for the cause of Christ in a century that has seen more Christian blood spilt than in all Church history combined, may be pre-teens who have not yet reached puberty. The apostles and prophets who will bring in the greatest harvest in the history of mankind may be unrecognizable today as they ride their tricycles down our driveways. Surely these are worthy of the most costly investments we can make!

Men and women of God, may your sacrifices and your obedience to God in pursuing your inheritance and in passing it on to the next generation give life to all with whom you come in contact. May the fire of your life demonstrate again and again that Elisha's bones still live!

Chapter 15

The Hinge of History: Raising Up Nazirites

A Unique Place in History

The people waited and wondered: What had happened to Zachariah? He had entered the Holy Place to burn incense before the Lord but had not returned. What could be delaying him?

Zachariah, meanwhile, was having the experience of a lifetime. An older man, he and his wife Elizabeth were without children. Imagine his profound shock when the angel Gabriel appeared to him and promised that his wife would bear a son, and that the boy's name would be John. It is not surprising that Zachariah asked Gabriel for a sign that the birth would occur. After all, it had been 400 years since Israel had been blessed with prophetic revelation. Now he was being told that he would father a prophet—and not just any prophet, but a Nazirite who would bear the mantle of the great Elijah!

And he will go on before the Lord, in the spirit and power of Elijah, to turn the hearts of the fathers to their children and the disobedient to the wisdom of the righteous—to make ready a people prepared for the Lord (Luke 1:17).

No wine or liquor was to touch John's lips, and no scissors his hair, the sign of consecration as a Nazirite. He would be filled with the Holy Spirit even from his mother's womb, being consecrated to the Lord all his life. Indeed, John was certainly an extraordinary person! Spending most of his time in the wilderness, he became a clear voice calling his people back to God. He prepared the way for the clearest unveiling of God that mankind has ever seen: the presence of the eternal God in physical form! Jesus said of him, "I tell you the truth: Among those born of women there has not risen anyone greater than John the Baptist..." (Mt. 11:11).

Gabriel alludes to the words of the prophet Malachi when he speaks to Zachariah in the Holy Place.[1] Yet he doesn't quote Malachi exactly. He says that the disobedient will be turned to the wisdom of the righteous. If ever there was a disobedient generation in need of being turned back to righteousness, it's Generation X. This generation has more knowledge than any other generation in history, yet they completely lack the wisdom of the righteous. Having been conceived in rejection and baptized with a flood of filth greater than anything that has come before, they desperately need a voice calling them to repentance.

What God has done once, He will do again. Even as John called his generation to prepare for the physical coming of Jesus, so God is raising up young people who will prepare the earth for the second coming of our Lord. The Lord is jealous for this generation that has been written off by much of mankind. Before the great and terrible day of the Lord, He will surely call these young people back to the wisdom of righteousness. Even now He is raising youth and young adults to carry the mantle of John and issue the call. They are to be called Generation Xploits!

God is again looking for Nazirites who will open the door for the next move of God. This responsibility may rest on one man or woman. Or there may be many. Whether one or many, Generation X is to be the hinge upon which all history hangs.

My generation and the generation of my parents are not crazy enough to carry this mantle, but Generation X is. They have seen everything that money can buy and are sick of it. They are ready for something else. They are a generation poised to say, "We will do the extreme thing."

If you are part of Generation X, you occupy a unique place on the timeline of history. You have been precisely positioned to accomplish God's victory in this hour. John prepared the Jewish nation for the unveiling of Jesus, "the Lamb of God, who takes away the sin of the world!" (Jn. 1:29) You will prepare the nations of the earth for the magnificent return of the Lion of Judah, "who will judge the living and the dead" (2 Tim. 4:1).

You live in a season of history that your forefathers would have longed to see. To miss what God is doing now is to miss everything. Find out what God is doing in your generation and give yourself to it. David did this: "For when David had served God's purpose in his own generation, he fell asleep..." (Acts 13:36). So must you, for in every generation and dispensation, there is something that God wants to do. To miss it, is to miss the purpose of God for your life!

I've lived for years with a Christianity that lacked power. When the Spirit of God began to pour out in 1994, I decided that I would rather dive into this river and risk all, than to stand shivering on the banks, wondering if this was from God or not. Since then, I've seen more fruit in 4 years than I had in 20!

I remember when some Japanese international students in our church started inviting their friends to renewal meetings. Several of these young men and women were Buddhists, and most had never been inside a church before. When we'd ask them if they wanted to accept Jesus, they'd say no. However, when they would stand on the prayer lines and we would pray for them, they'd be knocked down by the power of the Holy Spirit—many without anyone touching them. When they got up, they were ready to receive Christ! Had we wavered in the day of visitation, I would have missed the purposes of God.

God's Answer to National Distress and Spiritual Decay

Nazirites are special people. As the Old Testament reveals, God raises them up when His people are in great distress because they have succumbed to spiritual and moral decay. Time and time again throughout Israel's history, Nazirites turned the tide of spiritual and national degeneration.

Samson was such a man.[2] The angel who announced his birth to his parents proclaimed that Samson would deliver Israel from their dreaded enemies the Philistines. Not only was he to let his hair grow long and to abstain from wine, strong drink, and unclean food from birth to death, but his mother was also commanded to remain pure so that even from the womb the child would be consecrated to the Lord. This devotion to Yahweh, symbolized by Samson's long hair, was the source of Samson's great strength. Again and again he defeated the Philistines through the power of the Lord's Spirit. In the end, however, immorality claimed Samson and his consecration to the Lord ended when his hair was cut. Then his great strength left him and the Philistines afflicted him.

The days of Eli the priest were another time of moral and spiritual darkness in Israel. The priesthood had degenerated under Eli, who did nothing to discipline his two sons when they desecrated the sacrifices and slept with the women who served at the entrance to the Tent of Meeting.[3] Because of this corruption, God swore that no one from Eli's house would serve Him again as priest. In Eli's place God raised up Samuel. Holy from childhood, Samuel was God's response to a woman's desperate plea to become a mother. Samuel became the only man to serve Israel as judge, prophet, and priest.[4]

America is now in a time of national crisis. Moral and spiritual degeneration abound. From our birth, God called us to be a nation set apart unto Him, a city set on a hill, blessing the whole world. Then, like Samson, we began to sell ourselves to sexual immorality. Now our hair has been cut and we've lost our strength. But just as Samson's hair grew back, so America is once again remembering the source of her strength. Young people across the country are saying, "Give us one more chance. We want to rip down the pillars at the gates of hell and see the enemies that have ravaged our generation destroyed."

Nazirites, arise! May God be pleased to answer your prayers, remembering America even as He remembered Samson and strengthened him to kill more Philistines in his death than in all the days of his life. May God respond to you, our youth, because of the dedication and faithfulness of our forefathers.

A Vow of Purity

In Old Testament times, the uncut hair of a Nazirite symbolized his consecration to the Lord. Nazirites today may not bear this mark of consecration, but they are still called to live with a purpose and purity that cannot be mistaken. They are to be totally set apart for the Lord's holy purpose.

Wine was an acceptable beverage in the days of Samson and Samuel—although drunkenness was not! Still, Nazirites voluntarily gave up wine—even grapes and raisins, from which wine can be derived. This standard of purity is needed today in America. It is a purity that freely chooses to abstain from what is acceptable, for the purpose of gaining what is otherwise unobtainable. Many forms of entertainment are acceptable today. There is no end to the books, television shows, computer games, videos, and movies that fill our minds with filth. Some would argue that they are strong enough not to be affected by the R-rated movies they watch. What nonsense! Satan relentlessly battles to claim our souls.

Nazirites, arise. It's time to make war on the god of entertainment that has enticed and bound America. Separate yourselves from the lusts of this world. Obey God's Word to abstain from the fleshly lusts that wage war within. Then may your minds be filled with God's wisdom, so that you may mature into the mind of Christ and lead the Church in the paths of righteousness.

No Legalistic "Corpses" Allowed!

The rule concerning Nazirites and the dead was very severe. Nazirites were not allowed to touch even their own parents when they died, and a Nazirite's hair was to be cut immediately should someone die in his presence.

This rule speaks to me of legalism and dead works. Many Christians today are bound by forms of godliness that lack power because they are but traditions and not the commandments of God. This was the condition of the Pharisees when John the Baptist came preaching repentance.

A Nazirite and a Pharisee shared much in common: Both were zealous for God. Both fasted frequently. Both lived in separation and purity. Yet John, the greatest Nazirite of all, did not commend the Pharisees for their piety. He fiercely rebuked them. Why? They were filled with self-righteousness. They considered John's baptism for repentance to be an insult. After all, it was Gentile converts who needed such a baptism—or so the Pharisees thought. Had they submitted to John's baptism, they would have been admitting that their carefully constructed religious system was somehow incomplete, that their rigid adherence to the Law was not enough, that they were indeed no better than the Gentiles they despised! So the Pharisees rejected God's work through John.

> (All the people, even the tax collectors, when they heard Jesus' words, acknowledged that God's way was right, because they had been baptized by John. But the Pharisees and experts in the law rejected God's purpose for themselves, because they had not been baptized by John) (Lk. 7:29-30).

Jesus was no more complimentary to the Pharisees than John had been. John called them a "brood of vipers."[5] Jesus said that they were like "whitewashed tombs, which look beautiful on the outside but on the inside are full of dead men's bones and everything unclean" (Mt. 23:27). What an indictment!

The Church in America is often no different today. We appear to be spiritual, but we are only religious. We honor our traditions and miss God. As a young man I missed the Jesus Movement because I was religious. Signs and wonders were taking place all around me, and people were getting saved. But like the Pharisees who missed God when Jesus was right in front of their eyes, I missed God when the Jesus Movement swept through California. In fact, I left one Jesus People meeting in an angry mood, cursing God for what was happening there. I was the leader of my youth group, but I had no spiritual desire. I was not hungry for God.

Nazirites, arise! May your spiritual hunger cause you to embrace what God is doing in this hour. May you separate yourselves from anything that would cause you to honor Him with your lips, but keep Him at a distance in your hearts. May your worship be pure and holy unto the Lord from hearts that reverence God alone and are not bound by the rules of men.

Nazirites Deny Themselves the Pleasures of the Flesh

Nazirites fasted often. John the Baptist ate only locusts and honey. The impact of his fasting is shown in the power of his ministry. Prophets are forged in the desert of fasting, not in the desserts of feasting.

For years I have felt that God called me to a lifestyle of fasting. One time I prayed, "God, give me a sign that I'm going to be a Nazirite." The next day an Asian teen came to me and said, "I had a dream about you last night that you had long, long hair." Again I prayed, "Lord, give me *another* sign, please." The next day a junior high youth walked up to my house and asked me, "Lou, what's a Nazirite? I was reading the Book of Numbers when God spoke to me and said that I was to be a Nazirite." Today he's growing his hair. He's strange—and I love him.

God is again raising up youth who are more concerned with honoring and serving the Lord than with meeting the desires of their flesh. They will influence their world because of the strength of their desire. I was reminded of this principle when I was reading *Fasting for Spiritual Breakthrough* by Elmer L. Towns. Towns says,

"Begin the John the Baptist fast knowing the kind of influence you want to be. Remember, there are not only positive and negative influences, but also degrees of influence. On a scale of 1 to 10, Phil may be a 7, Kara may only be a 2. Much of the difference among these depends on desire.

"… Although the angel told John's father, Zacharias, that John was to accept a Nazirite vow, that decision had to be decided and confirmed by John. There is power in that kind of decision—one that controls your life. You must make a decision to serve God, then you must daily make that decision work."[6]

As I read, I first said, "Oh God, don't say that to me! Don't make me live a fasted lifestyle." Then I read more and saw that John led a whole movement of God, being a hinge of history. Then I said, "But God, I want to do that."

A few days after reading this, I preached at a Rock the Nations conference. Gary Black was also speaking. He said, "You could have an influence of a 2 or a 7 or a 10 according to your desire. John the Baptist had a great desire and began to pray and fast—and he influenced a whole nation." I was completely stunned. *Gary must have read that book*, I thought. When the altar call was given, I was the first one to the altar. Later I asked Gary if he had read Towns' book. "Never read it," he replied.

America is intoxicated with the pleasures of this world. We say that we are hungry, but we don't know what hunger is! We have become slaves of food, the granddaddy of all appetites. In the words of the apostle Paul, "…[our] god is [our] stomach, and [our] glory is in [our] shame" (Phil. 3:19a).

An intercessor told me about a dream in which a snake coiled around a donut. This may sound strange to you, but it wasn't very funny to me! Every morning I'd wake up to two calls: a call from the House of Prayer and a call from the donut shop saying, "Lou, come. Maple bars." Many a morning the maple bars won. When I heard this dream, I felt the Lord say, "There is a coiling serpent around the donut because when you give in to those pleasures, you begin to get morally weak in every other area." Ezekiel's accusation against the city of Sodom seems to support this. The sin of Sodom was not only homosexuality but also overeating and arrogance.[7] Sexual perversions abounded in the city because these things flourish in a self-indulgent society.

Consecration to God and self-indulgence cannot live together. Love for God must supersede everything else. Pure love births a desire to give that finds pleasure simply in the giving. Its focus is on the affection of the Lover, not the approval of men. It knows no humiliation or shame and does not consider the cost.

The woman who wept over Jesus' feet and anointed them with costly perfume loved her Lord.[8] She hardly noticed the scandalized Pharisees or the cost of her seeming extravagance. Her act was a gift of love, not a show to impress.

Love makes even great cost and sacrifice seem insignificant—even a joy. My kids demonstrated this when they had no gift to give me for my birthday and so brought me their favorite baseball cards. They were so happy to give me their best cards! To them it was no sacrifice at all because they love me. This is love, not legalism. Love gets the best in the house and pours it out on the beloved.

Nazirites, arise! May you serve the Lord from a heart of love, loving Him because He first loved you,[9] and may you thereby avoid the deadly traps of legalism and self-indulgence.

Leaders in Battle

True Nazirites are strong in battle. Having won the battle against the lusts of the flesh, they are able to stand in the day of evil. Proverbs 25:28 affirms this truth: "Like a city whose walls are broken down is a man who lacks self-control." In other words, a person with no self-control is defenseless and vulnerable to attack. He has nothing with which to shield himself.

In the days of the judges in Israel, it was the practice of soldiers to let their hair uncut before going into battle. An alternate translation for the first part of Deborah's song of victory seems to refer to this practice: "When the princes in Israel take the lead, [When long locks of hair hung loose in Israel], when the people willingly offer themselves—praise the Lord!" (Judg. 5:2)[10] This was an allusion to the Nazirite consecration. It spoke of the soldiers' complete dedication to the battle. It was the longhaired champions who led in the battle! Then the people willingly followed.

Youth of America, it's time to let your hair down. May you be "arrayed in holy majesty, from the womb of the dawn [and may] you...receive the dew of your youth" (Ps. 110:3b).[11]

Phenomenal Influence

When I was just two years old in the Lord, I was sitting in a theater watching a movie that mocked God. The Holy Spirit spoke to me, saying, "Stand up, Lou, in the middle of this theater and tell them that I don't need this kind of help. Tell them to turn to Jesus Christ if they want to know the true God." I said no to the Lord. Suddenly it became like fire in my bones and the next thing I knew, I found myself preaching in front of the movie theater: "If you want to know the true God, turn to Jesus Christ." I preached, then ran like crazy, crying hard because I was scared to death! The next day someone walked up to one of my friends and said, "You wouldn't believe it, but last night I was at this movie theater, and this wild guy stood up and started preaching."

God is looking for wild men and women who will live the Christian life to the hilt with a fearless devotion to Him. These consecrated ones, like John the Baptist, will be "great in the sight of the Lord" (Lk. 1:15). They will be bright and shining lights[12] who are not cowed by public opinion or the demands of religious tradition—and their influence will be phenomenal.

John the Baptist lived in obscurity on the fringe of society. Yet his few short years of ministry and his controversial message shook the Jewish nation[13]—and actually scared the king. (Josephus, the Jewish historian, tells us that Herod actually feared John because of his tremendous social and spiritual influence.[14]) John was not preaching in an air-conditioned auditorium or the palaces of his day, yet some estimate that 750,000 people went out to the desert to hear John during the 18 months of his preaching. That's 40,000 to 50,000 people a month! That's like Pensacola!

Nazirites, arise! May you be great in the sight of the Lord as you seek His approval rather than the admiration of men. Refuse to live by society's quirks and demands. Exert peer pressure instead of responding to it. Then may influence like that of John the Baptist be yours, turning our world to God.

Nazirites Are Dedicated to the Lord By Their Parents

Parents, God's call for Nazirites is not just for the kids. Samson, Samuel, and John were all born to mothers who had been barren. They were set apart from their births, dedicated to the Lord. Their parents knew that they were to be raised as Nazirites, and they honored the Lord in this. The prayer of Manoah, Samson's father, should be in the heart of every parent of Generation X and the millennial generation youth: "O Lord, I beg You, let the man of God You sent to us come again to teach us how to bring up the boy who is to be born" (Judg. 13:8b). Likewise, Samson's mother obeyed the angel who instructed her to take the Nazirite oath while she was pregnant, for it takes purity to deliver purity. Oh, for this same consecration to fill the hearts of mothers today!

Arise, parents and leaders of the coming Nazirite generation. Sanctify yourselves to raise kids who will deliver our land from impending judgment. May we be a new breed of parents and spiritual guardians who walk before the Lord in purity and integrity, honoring Him in how we live and in how we raise our kids.

Judgment Comes on Those Who Defile a Nazirite

A man of God who has been involved in missions once told me the story of a young girl who was deeply stirred by his preaching on missions. One day she came up to him and said, "I want to go to missions so bad I can feel it in my heart, but my mom wants me to go to college. She won't let me go." So the girl never went to the mission field. Within four years she had fallen into sexual immorality and was totally backslidden from serving the Lord. Her mother came to this same man and asked him if he could help her daughter. His sad but honest reply was, "It's your fault. When she wanted to run in the purposes of God, you said no."

This mother is reaping the sad consequences described in Amos 2:11-13:

> *"I also raised up prophets from among your sons and Nazirites from among your young men. Is this not true, people of Israel?" declares the Lord. "But you made the Nazirites drink wine and commanded the prophets not to prophesy. Now then, I will crush you...."*

She is not alone. There is a judgment on America right now because we have told our sons and daughters not to prophesy, dream, see visions, or speak in tongues.

This must change! God is touching our youth and using them to bring America to repentance. I know a nice evangelical girl who came to our church two years ago. The Holy Spirit fell on her and she began to speak in tongues—in Mandarin! People were converted when she told them in Mandarin that they needed to turn their lives around!

Church of America, arise! We must release our young prophets or we will be crushed. May God give us a vision for liberating our sons and daughters to reach the nations! May we recognize the call of God on their lives, encourage a sacrificial consecration, and make no demands on them that God is not making. May we give our best, our children, as our love gift to the Lord.

Then may they walk in the ways of our forefathers, dying, perhaps, to reach the Muslims, Buddhists, Hindus, and other peoples to whom the Lord sends them. And may they walk in the way of John the Baptist, who never opened a blind eye or raised a dead man, but raised a dead nation!

We stand on the threshold of a time in history like no other. In the darkest hour America has ever known, God is about to act. He's raising up Nazirites. The long prophetic silence is ending. In a generation given over to immorality, when the priesthood is defiled, the cry of the word of the Lord is again being heard in our land. Not one, but thousands of John the Baptists with the spirit of Elijah stand poised to change our world. The purity of their lives shines and the passion of their hearts blazes. The hour for these long-haired champions to burn brightly has come.

Rise up, oh Nazirite generation. Redig the wells of revival that have long been forgotten. And may the same spirit of consecration and the powerful, clean fear of the Lord fall on all of us mightily. May we be propelled by His Spirit to loose the gushers and geysers of our forefathers all across the land—for ourselves and for our children. And may the Lord Himself be provoked to show mercy to us in this *hour of Jubilee.*

Endnotes

Chapter 1

1. Derek Prince, *Shaping History Through Prayer and Fasting* (New Kensington, PA: Whitaker House, 1973), 133. Used by permission of the publisher, Whitaker House, 30 Hunt Valley Circle, New Kensington, PA 15068.

2. Frank Bartleman, *Azusa Street* (New Brunswick, NJ: Bridge-Logos Publishers, Inc., 1980), 46,53. Used by permission.

3. *Intercessors for America*, Vol. 20, No. 1, January 1993.

4. These are Hebraic years of 360 days rather than the Roman 365 days.

5. *Intercessors for America*, Vol. 20, No. 1, January 1993.

6. Rick Joyner, "The Morning Star Prophetic Bulletin," June 1998.

7. "Porn Pays," *Los Angeles Daily News*, Business Section, November 20, 1997.

8. I [Rick Joyner] have told people to seek the Lord and leave [southern California] only if He directs them to. However, I have been told that the time is coming soon when I will have to begin telling people that they should only stay if they hear from the Lord to stay.

I also personally feel that I am to invest in some kind of retreat property in southern California. I have been told that I am not to abandon the area, and that I must be willing to spend time there doing what I can to help the church in that region. Regardless of where we live, we are making a terrible mistake if we think that this is southern California's problem and not our problem too. When this happens, it will be devastating to the whole world. We are all members of one body, and this is the most important time for us to stand with the church in that region and to intercede for all the people of southern California. It is not God's desire for any to perish, but for all to be saved and come to the knowledge of truth.

The safest place in the world is in God's will, even if it is in the middle of a devastating earthquake. The most dangerous place in the world is to be out of His will. If you live in southern California and you leave out of God's will, you will be in danger. Our Armageddon can come at the next stoplight! As we proceed into the times ahead, it will become increasingly dangerous to be even a little bit out of God's will. The Lord is now giving us ample warning to hear from Him and obey Him.

9. Rick Joyner, "The Morning Star Prophetic Bulletin," June 1998.

10. See Genesis 18:20–19:25.

11. Mario Murillo, *Critical Mass* (Grand Rapids, MI: Anthony Douglas Publishing, 1985), xi. Used by permission.

12. See Leviticus 25:9.

Chapter 2

1. See Genesis 26:18.

2. Frank Bartleman, *Azusa Street* (New Brunswick, NJ: Bridge-Logos Publishers, Inc., 1980), 1. Used by permission.

3. See Second Kings 2.

4. Tommy Tenney, speaking at the Catch the Fire Conference at Harvest Rock Church, November 1997.

5. Renée DeLoriea, *Portal in Pensacola* (Shippensburg, PA: Revival Press, 1997), 15-16.

6. Story used with permission.

7. See Genesis 21:14-20.

8. See Genesis 26:20-22.

9. See Exodus 16:14-36.

10. See Genesis 37:22-24; Jeremiah 38:6; 41:7.

11. *Los Angeles Times*, March 20, 1998.

12. See John 4:14.

13. John Dawson, *Taking Our Cities for God: How to Break Spiritual Strongholds* (Lake Mary, FL: Creation House, 1989), 94. Used by permission.

Chapter 3

1. John Kilpatrick, *Feast of Fire* (Pensacola, FL: Self-published, 1995), 26.

2. John Dawson, *Taking Our Cities for God: How to Break Spiritual Strongholds* (Lake Mary, FL: Creation House, 1989), 92. Used by permission.

3. Carl Friedrich Keil and Franz Julius Delitzsch, *The Twelve Minor Prophets, Biblical Commentary on the Old Testament*, Vol. II (Edinburgh: T. & T. Clark, 1873), 472. Used by permission of Wm. B. Eerdmans Publishing Co.

4. Founder of Nazarenes.

5. Leader of Azusa Street Revival.

6. Founder of Gospel Light publishing house.

7. Founder of Foursquare Gospel Church.

8. Pioneer of revival crusades.

9. Founder of Campus Crusade for Christ.

10. Founder of Last Days Ministries.

11. Pioneer in the Charismatic Movement.

12. Founder of Full Gospel Business Men's Fellowship.

Chapter 4

1. George Otis, Jr., *The Last of the Giants* (Tarrytown, NY: Chosen Books, Inc., a division of Baker Book House Company, 1991), 157-158. Used by permission.

2. See Rick Joyner, *The World Aflame* (Charlotte, NC: MorningStar Publications, 1993), 35.

3. See Hebrews 5:7.

4. See First Chronicles 22:1ff.

5. Mario Murillo, *Critical Mass* (Grand Rapids, MI: Anthony Douglas Publishing, 1985), 46. Used by permission.

Chapter 5

1. See First Samuel 20:17.

2. See Genesis 17:10.

3. See Genesis 13:14-16.

4. See First Samuel 18:2-3.

5. John Dawson, *Taking Our Cities for God: How to Break Spiritual Strongholds* (Lake Mary, FL: Creation House, 1989), 92-93. Used by permission.

6. Francis Frangipane, *The River of Life* (New Kensington, PA: Whitaker House, 1993), 113. Used by permission of the publisher, Whitaker House, 30 Hunt Valley Circle, New Kensington, PA 15068.

7. See Isaiah 49:15-16.

Chapter 6

1. See Steve Hawthorne and Graham Kendrick, *Prayer-walking* (Lake Mary, FL: Creation House, 1993).

2. Msgr. Francis J. Weber, *The Life and Times of Fray Junípero Serra* (EZ Nature Books, San Luis Obispo, 1988), 21-22.

2. Weber, *The Life and Times*, 25.

4. Weber, *The Life and Times*, 28.

5. Weber, *The Life and Times*, 40.

6. Weber, *The Life and Times*, 50.

7. As quoted in Weber, *The Life and Times*, 50.

8. Weber, *The Life and Times*, 50.

9. See Richard Gazoski, *The Prophetic Whisper* (San Francisco, CA: Voice of Pentecost, Inc., 1996), 30.

10. David Matthews, "I Saw the Welsh Revival," *The Double Outburst*, November 1904, as quoted in R.B. Jones, *Rent Heavens*.

11. See Genesis 11:1-9.

12. See Ezekiel 1:1; Acts 7:56; 10:11.

13. See Mark 1:10.

14. James Strong, *Strong's Exhaustive Concordance of the Bible* (Peabody, MA: Hendrickson Publishers, n.d.), G4977.

15. See Revelation 4:1.

Chapter 7

1. Frank Bartleman, *Another Wave of Revival* (New Kensington, PA: Whitaker House, 1982), 8-9. Used by permission of the publisher, Whitaker House, 30 Hunt Valley Circle, New Kensington, PA 15068.

2. Frank Bartleman, *Azusa Street* (New Brunswick, NJ: Bridge-Logos Publishers, Inc., 1980), 47. Used by permission.

3. See Bartleman, *Azusa Street*, 47.

4. Based on an account in Rick Joyner, "Azusa—The Fire That Would Not Die," *MorningStar Journal*, Vol. 7, No. 1.

5. See Isaiah 62:6-7.

6. Mario Murillo, *Critical Mass* (Grand Rapids, MI: Anthony Douglas Publishing, 1985), 4-5. Used by permission.

7. John Dawson, *Taking Our Cities for God: How to Break Spiritual Strongholds* (Lake Mary, FL: Creation House, 1989), 94. Used by permission.

8. See Luke 15:11-32.

9. Rueben Martinez, *Los Angeles Times*, Opinion, March 29, 1998, M1,M3.

Chapter 8

1. Roberta H. Winter, *Once More Around Jericho: The Story of the U.S. Center for World Mission* (South Pasadena, CA: William Carey Library, 1978), 29. Used by permission.

2. Winter, *Once More*, 30.

3. Winter, *Once More*, 171.

4. Winter, *Once More*, 46.

5. Derek Prince, *Shaping History Through Prayer and Fasting* (New

Kensington, PA: Whitaker House, 1973), 215. Used by permission of the publisher, Whitaker House, 30 Hunt Valley Circle, New Kensington, PA 15068.

    6. See Genesis 28:4 KJV.

    7. See Genesis 26:12.

    8. Aimee Semple McPherson with Raymond L. Cox, *Aimee: Life Story of Aimee Semple McPherson* (Los Angeles, CA: Foursquare Publications, 1979), 111-112. Copyrighted by Heritage Department of the International Church of the Foursquare Gospel. Used by permission.

    9. See Genesis 28:13-15; 35:10-12.

    10. See Judges 20:18,21-28; 21:1-4.

    11. See Judges 4:4-5; First Samuel 7:15-16.

    12. See First Kings 12:26-29.

    13. See First Kings 16:31; 22:51-52; Second Kings 3:1-3; 10:29-31; 13:1-2,10-11; 14:23-24; 15:8-9,17-18,24,27-28.

    14. See Jeremiah 48:13; Amos 3–5; Hosea 10–12.

    15. See First Kings 21:7-19.

Chapter 9

    1. *Star News,* Pasadena, California, 1947.

    2. "Pasadena Focus."

    3. See Second Kings 3:16-24.

    4. See Second Kings 6:1-7; 4:38-41; 4:1-7.

    5. Richard Riss, *A Survey of 20th-Century Revival Movements in North America* (Peabody, MA: Hendrickson Publishers, 1988), 126. Baldwin and Benson quote taken from *Henrietta Mears and How She Did It!* (Glendale, CA: Gospel Light Publications, 1966), 232. Used by permission.

    6. Riss, *A Survey,* 128-130,142-143. Quote from Baldwin and Benson, *Henrietta Mears,* 250.

Chapter 10

    1. See Daniel 1:20.

    2. Derek Prince, *Shaping History Through Prayer and Fasting* (New Kensington, PA: Whitaker House, 1973), 31. Used by permission of the publisher, Whitaker House, 30 Hunt Valley Circle, New Kensington, PA 15068.

    3. See Daniel 9:1-19.

    4. See Daniel 10.

    5. See First Samuel 3:9-10.

    6. See Luke 2:25-38.

    7. Frank Bartleman, *Another Wave of Revival* (New Kensington, PA: Whitaker House, 1982), 17,28. Used by permission of the publisher, Whitaker House, 30 Hunt Valley Circle, New Kensington, PA 15068.

    8. See Prince, *Shaping History,* 140.

    9. See Daniel 6.

    10. Mario Murillo, *Critical Mass* (Grand Rapids, MI: Anthony Douglas Publishing, 1985), 25. Used by permission.

    11. See also Romans 8:14-30.

    12. Murillo, *Critical Mass,* 21-24.

    13. Paraphrased from an article by Paul Cain, "Shiloh Newsletter," Vol. 1, No. 1.

14. Walter Wink, "History Belongs to the Intercessors," *Sojourners*, October 1990. Reprinted in George Otis, Jr., *Last of the Giants* (Tarrytown, NY: Chosen Books, 1991).

Chapter 11

1. Mario Murillo, *Critical Mass* (Grand Rapids, MI: Anthony Douglas Publishing, 1985), 25. Used by permission.

2. Franklin Hall, *The Fasting Prayer* (Phoenix AZ: Hall Deliverance Foundation, Inc., 1947, 1976), 26. Used by permission.

3. Gordon Lindsey, spoken message in 1997.

4. Ern Hawtin, as quoted in Richard Riss, *Latter Rain* (Honeycomb Visual Productions Ltd, 1987), 60. Used by permission.

5. "A Call to Fast, in Hopes of a Spiritual Revival," *New York Times*.

6   See Matthew 4:1-2.

7. See Acts 1:14.

8. See Acts 13:2-3.

9. Hall, *The Fasting Prayer*, 25. See also Acts 1:14.

10. Hall, *The Fasting Prayer*, 25.

11. See Romans 11:22.

12. "A Call to Fast, in Hopes of a Spiritual Revival," *New York Times*.

13. Derek Prince, *Shaping History Through Prayer and Fasting* (New Kensington, PA: Whitaker House, 1973), 143. Used by permission of the publisher, Whitaker House, 30 Hunt Valley Circle, New Kensington, PA 15068.

14. See Matthew 11:12.

15. See Proverbs 29:18 KJV.

16. See Habbakuk 2:2 KJV.

17. See Ecclesiastes 4:9-10.

18. See Daniel 10:1-2.

19. See Matthew 6:18.

20. Shared in a personal conversation with the author.

Chapter 13

1. See Romans 4:17.

2. James Strong, *Strong's Exhaustive Concordance of the Bible* (Peabody, MA: Hendrickson Publishers, n.d.), H3041.

3. See Luke 1:66, which records the naming of John the Baptist.

4. A.W. Clemenhage, *History of the Brethren in Christ Church* (Nappanee, IN: E.V. Publishing House, 1952), 347-348. Used by permission.

5. See Psalm 42:1.

6. See Genesis 27:27-40.

7. See Genesis 49:1-27.

8. See First Chronicles 4:9-10.

9. See Psalm 139.

10. See Luke 2:42-49.

Chapter 14

1. See First Kings 13:2.

2. See also Romans 11:16-26. In this book, I have discussed mainly the

ancient wells and covenants of revival in recent years. However, the original wells and covenants are all Jewish, which might be the topic of another book.

3. See Zechariah 4:1-6.

4. See Revelation 1:20.

5. Frank Damazio, speaking at the Catch the Fire Conference at Harvest Rock Church, November 14, 1997.

6. See First Kings 19:15-16.

7. Edward A. Elliot, "His Mysterious Ways," *Guideposts,* June 1990.

Chapter 15

1. See Malachi 4:6.

2. See Judges 13–14.

3. See First Samuel 2:22.

4. See First Samuel 1.

5. See Matthew 3:7; 12:34; 23:33.

6. Elmer L. Towns, *Fasting for Spiritual Breakthrough* (Ventura, CA: Regal Books, 1996), 149. Used by permission.

7. See Ezekiel 16:49.

8. See Luke 7:37-50.

9. See First John 4:19.

10. See Arthur Cundall, *Judges and Ruth—An Introduction and Commentary* (Leicester, England: InterVarsity Press, 1968), 94.

11. The last phrase can also read: "your young men will come to you like the dew."

12. See John 5:35 KJV.

13. See Mark 1:5.

14. Josephus, *Antiquities of the Jews,* Book XVIII, Chapter V, page 2. Translated by William Whiston. Published 1867.

Other

Destiny Image titles
you will enjoy reading

THE LOST PASSIONS OF JESUS
by Donald L. Milam, Jr.
What motivated Jesus to pursue the cross? What inner strength kept His feet on the path laid before Him? Time and tradition have muted the Church's knowledge of the passions that burned in Jesus' heart, but if we want to—if we dare to—we can still seek those same passions. Learn from a close look at Jesus' own life and words and from the writings of other dedicated followers the passions that enflamed the Son of God and changed the world forever!
ISBN 0-9677402-0-7

FATHER, FORGIVE US!
by Jim W. Goll.
What is holding back a worldwide "great awakening"? What hinders the Church all over the world from rising up and bringing in the greatest harvest ever known? The answer is simple: sin! God is calling Christians today to take up the mantle of identificational intercession and repent for the sins of the present and past; for the sins of our fathers; for the sins of the nations. Will you heed the call? This book shows you how!
ISBN 0-7684-2025-3

THE MARTYRS' TORCH
by Bruce Porter.
In every age of history, darkness has threatened to extinguish the light. But also in every age of history, heroes and heroines of the faith rose up to hold high the torch of their testimony—witnesses to the truth of the gospel of Jesus Christ. On a fateful spring day at Columbine High, others lifted up their torches and joined the crimson path of the martyrs' way. We cannot forget their sacrifice. A call is sounding forth from Heaven: "Who will take up the martyrs' torch which fell from these faithful hands?" Will you?
ISBN 0-7684-2046-6

PROPHETIC MINISTRIES
by T. Austin Sparks.
What is God's purpose for His Church today? How can believers know and fulfill that purpose? Biblical prophets called God's people to clear spiritual vision and holy living. The need for holiness is as urgent for today's Church as it was for the Old Testament Jews. This reprint of a classic book by the late T. Austin Sparks, a British pastor, paints a fresh picture of the prophet and challenges the Body of Christ to once again proclaim God's presence among the nations of the world!
ISBN 0-7684-4000-9

Available at your local Christian bookstore.

Internet: http://www.reapernet.com